# CHRIST AND THE CHURCH

# Christ and the Church

*In Orthodox Teaching and Tradition*

Archbishop Gregory Afonsky

ST VLADIMIR'S SEMINARY PRESS
CRESTWOOD, NEW YORK 10707
2001

Library of Congress Cataloging-in-Publication Data

Afonsky, Gregory, 1925-

Christ and the church in Orthodox teaching and tradition / Gregory Afonsky.

p.   cm.

Includes bibliographical references.

ISBN 0-88141-216-3 (alk. paper)

1. Church   2. Jesus Christ—Person and offices.   3. Orthodox Eastern Church—Doctrines.   I. Title.

BX323 .A48 2001

262'.019—dc21

2001019143

# Christ and the Church
# In Orthodox Teaching and Tradition

St Vladimir's Seminary Press
575 Scarsdale Road, Crestwood NY 10707
1-800-204-2665


ISBN 0-88141-216-3

# Contents

# Preface

This book is the fruit of more than thirty years of study, reflection, and teaching. Its purpose is to explain as clearly as possible the divine origin, nature, authority and life of the Orthodox Church. It examines aspects of the faith which contemporary members of the Church may not have contemplated previously.

Through contact with many believers, including students of theology, it has become evident to me that most people are familiar with the objective truth of Orthodoxy and recognize what our Lord Jesus Christ has done for fallen man as their savior, redeemer, sanctifier, and moral example. These truths are well known, firmly believed and, it seems, readily and graciously accepted as God's free gifts to each person and to mankind as a whole. Yet, because Christianity is often understood to be the sum of all teaching of and about Jesus Christ, it is sometimes thought that as objective teaching it can exist without the Church, as a kind of "churchless Christianity." In fact, it was the Church of Christ which gave birth and life to Christianity. Indeed, the divine, saving gifts of our Savior Jesus Christ are manifested on earth *within* His Church (Mt 16:18).

Less clear and less understood is our subjective, personal response to all the gifts with which we Christians are endowed by God. Is it really enough for any Christian simply to accept the saving acts of God by faith alone, without obedience to His moral commandments and participation in Christ's sufferings, death, resurrection and ascension? Is it not essential to follow in His footsteps, to carry His cross, to incorporate into our lives all the divine gifts of God the Father, Son, and Holy Spirit, in order to become holy as God the Father is holy, and to grow to the measure of the stature of Jesus Christ in spiritual perfection? Here, we are clearly facing a dilemma as to where our path of salvation, the road to the Kingdom of God, lies.

Existing in a non-Orthodox world, surrounded by secular culture, exposed to arbitrary, subjective and one-sided interpretations of the Holy Scriptures, we are often tempted by the simplistic solution: either salvation "by faith alone," or, no less simplistic, "by the liturgy alone." From these perspectives the place of the Church concerning the process of salvation has not been clearly or positively expressed. In fact, identification of the Church with its founder and head, Jesus Christ, is often simply absent in discussions concerning the nature of the Christian community. For many people, the Church and Jesus Christ are two separate realities. Comments concerning the Church often reflect either a wholly non-Orthodox theology or a thoroughly secularized philosophy. For example, notions that the Church is simply another worldly institution with its own traditions or that the Church is a formalistic organization governed by a professional clergy, are commonplace.

During my twenty years of teaching in a theological seminary, each new academic year brought a variety of questions raised by the entering students. Do we need the Church? Is it not enough to live as the Holy Scriptures teach us? In the Scriptures we find a beautiful image of Christ, and His purity attracts us. Do we really need complicated dogmas, canons, elaborate services, as well as ongoing struggles to defend the Church against division and schism? Can't we simply pray peacefully at home, apart from the Church?

Upon hearing such questions, any true Orthodox Christian feels sorrow and concern for the future life of the Orthodox Church in our modern world. While firmly preserving a personal faith in our Lord and Savior Jesus Christ, we must not lose sight of the fact that the only way to participate in the life of Christ and to follow Him into the Kingdom of Heaven is *through* His Holy Church. For Christ is inseparably united to the Church, as its founder, foundation, and head. The Church is His body, the *fullness of Christ*, "the *fullness* of Him who fills all in all" (Eph 1:23).

Animated by the Holy Spirit, the Church is the source and locus of divine-human life, which begins at baptism and comes to fulfillment at *theosis*, or deification, within the Kingdom of God. Human ignorance, pride, and the desire to determine our own criteria as to what constitutes the religious and moral life lead us to miss the significance of the Church for our salvation. Yet the Church of the living God is the "pillar and bulwark of truth" (1 Tim 3:15) which alone prescribes the way and the means to piety and the moral life for us. It is *in* and *through* the Church that her faithful members inherit the Kingdom of God.

The most important task for Orthodox Christians is to attain salvation—the restoration of sonship with God to the point of deification—participation in the very life of God. This involves our participation in God's perfect love, life, and unity; our moral and spiritual perfection to reflect the perfect holiness of God the Father; together with our spiritual and physical perfection to the "measure of the stature of the fullness of Jesus Christ" (Eph 4:13). This pathway to eternal life and communion with God is made available in the one, holy, catholic, apostolic, Orthodox Church.

With the help of God, basing my research on the Holy Scriptures and Holy Tradition, and relying on numerous published works on ecclesiology in the Orthodox tradition, I have concentrated on the following themes: the divine plan of salvation, divine-human life in the Holy Trinity, the Church and the Kingdom of God, the Church of Jesus Christ and the apostles, the essential qualities of the Church, the Church as guardian and teacher of truth, and the life of the Church.

## *Acknowledgments*

This study is dedicated to the memory of Professor Sergei S. Verhovskoy, who encouraged me to concentrate on the field of ecclesiology, Professor A. Bogolepov, and our beloved professors at St Vladimir's Seminary, Protopresbyter Alexander Schmemann and Protopresbyter John Meyendorff.

An extensive bibliography is provided with the hope of encouraging further study in this complex and most important subject of ecclesiology, so dear to the heart of every Orthodox Christian.

The author wishes to express his deepest appreciation and gratitude to Archpriest John Breck, Ph.D. and Minadora Jacobs for editing and preparing the manuscript for publication.

Archbishop GREGORY (Afonsky)

August 1, 1998

Day of the Relics of St Seraphim of Sarov

# I

# Introduction

*"This *is* none other but the house of God, and this
*is* the gate of heaven" (Gen 28:17)*

Since the foundation of the Church, theological minds have tried to
define her essence and essential qualities. The aim has not been to
discern the innermost mystery of the Church, but to examine the divine origin and nature of the Body of Christ as revealed through
Holy Scripture and Church Tradition.[1] As Orthodox Christians, we
believe that the Holy Scriptures are inspired by God Himself and
that they reveal to us the way to salvation.

We also believe that the truth about God as the Orthodox
Church teaches it and the truth about God as revealed in the
Scriptures are one and the same; for the Source of truth, both in
the Scriptures and in the Church, is the one Holy Spirit. Our
knowledge of that truth, then, is provided both by the Scriptures
and by the Church.

An individual who interprets the Holy Scriptures in light of
his own subjective understanding can err, be deceived, or simply
exercise wrong judgment. The one, holy, catholic, apostolic Or-

---

[1] "The Holy Tradition is the living faith and teaching of the Ecumenical Church of
Christ." Thus, in the Orthodox Church, the Holy Tradition is understood to be the
whole teaching of the faith and life which the Church received from the same
God-inspired authority from which the Church received the Holy Scriptures. Being
of equal value concerning the truth, and acting in harmony and with equal author-
ity, the Holy Tradition is the first source of truth in the Church. It explains the
Holy Scriptures. At the same time, Holy Tradition is complemented by the Holy
Scriptures. For further reading on the subject of Holy Tradition as the source of
Christian knowledge, see: P.P. Ponomarev, *Sviashchennoe predanie, kak istochnik
Khristianskogo vedeniia* (Kazan, 1908), 544-555.

thodox Church, however, can never err, be deceived, or be wrong in her judgment, since the Church is infallible and forever the same in her nature as founded by God.[2]

The first and most significant dogma of the Orthodox Church concerns the Holy Trinity.[3] Two unique qualities distinguish this dogma—its absolute necessity for the existence of the Church and the absolute incomprehensibility of its essence.

The quality of "absolute necessity" lies in the fact that the dogma of the Holy Trinity contains within itself the whole essence of Christian faith, as well as the foundation for all teaching of and about Jesus Christ. As such the whole of Christian faith, as well as particular doctrinal teachings, depends upon and derives from the dogma of the Holy Trinity. This fact has special significance for Orthodox ecclesiology.

The quality of "absolute incomprehensibility" lies in the fact that the dogma of the Holy Trinity insists that the essence of the Holy Trinity—God's self-knowledge—is revealed to us neither in the Old nor the New Testament. We know that God exists and that He is the Creator (Gen 1:31); but what God is in His essence is not, and indeed, cannot be explained. We also know the Holy Trinity to be the divine life of one divine being (Mt 28:19), but the full mystery of the Trinity is inexplicable. Nevertheless, the

---

2  *Message of the Patriarchs of the Eastern-Catholic Church about the Orthodox Faith* (1723), no. 2.

3  The term "orthodox" signifies thinking correctly in matters of true faith, as opposed to incorrect belief, termed "heterodox" or in Greek *heterodoxos*. The term "dogma" or "doctrine"—also of Greek origin—can have various meanings: a firm conviction accepted by human reason, a royal decree, or the law of God. The Orthodox Church teaches that dogma/doctrine expresses the absolute truth of Christian faith and contains the following essential qualities: 1) dogma is the absolute, unchangeable and immutable truth of faith; 2) dogma is God's revealed truth, defined by the Church as the rule of faith under the guidance of the Holy Spirit and in the name of Jesus Christ; 3) dogma is the law of God for all members of the Orthodox Church. On doctrine in the Holy Scriptures, see especially Mt 7:28-29; Jn 7:16-17; 18:19; 1 Cor 14:26; Acts 17:19; 1 Tim 4:6 and 16; 6:3; 2 Tim 3:16; Titus 1:9; 2:1; 2 Jn 9. See also, N. Malinovskii, *Ocherk pravoslavnogo dogmaticheskogo bogosloviia* [Moscow]: Sergiev Posad, vol. 1, 4-8.

human intellect tries constantly to fathom this dogma, in order to understand and eventually explain these mysteries as far as the human mind is capable.

Thus, just as we cannot speak of the essence of the Holy Trinity, which is the foundation of the Church, so we cannot speak of our knowledge of the essence of the Church—its deepest inner meaning. Although, we can never know the true essence of the Church, we can perceive much about its nature through the revealed qualities of the Holy Trinity. These qualities are reflected as qualities of the Church itself and are made known to us through the Holy Scriptures, Holy Tradition, and in the teachings of the Church Fathers.

The doctrine of the Church is not the same as the "self-consciousness" or "self-expression" of the Church. Rather, it explains and describes the origin, nature, and life of the Church—her goal, purpose, and the means by which her purpose is fulfilled. The dogma also reveals how the Church differs from all that is *not* the Church, since the Church is not of natural, earthly origin. According to the clear teaching of our Savior Jesus Christ, the deep and mysterious life of the Church is permanently and unalterably animated by the divine life of Christ Himself and of the Holy Spirit. This divine, mysterious life of the Church cannot be logically defined. To understand the reality of the Church and her life, one must actually *participate* in that life as a member of the living organism, which is the Body of Christ.

In the Church's early history, various heresies such as Gnosticism, Montanism, Novatianism, and Donatism[4] tried to

4  These were the ecclesiastical heresies of the second to the fifth centuries: Gnosticism (from the Greek word *gnosis*, meaning knowledge) was essentially an eclectic mixture of eastern philosophy with Christianity. Gnosticism was one of the philosophical religions, whose adherents considered it to be the most perfect and who tried to find justification for themselves in Christianity. Montanism derived its name from the founder of the heresy, Montanus. He taught against the nature of the Church by proclaiming a "new prophecy" in the appearance of the Paraclete (Comforter). The Donatists, or the "pure ones" raised a question concerning the holiness of the Church. Their idea was that the Church that accepts "lapsed" or fallen bishops into

pervert and distort a true understanding of the inner reality of the
Church. Similarly, in our own day, schismatic or heretical groups
are trying to present false understandings of the Church. Secular-
ism, relativism, and neo-Donatism bring confusion and false-
hoods to the minds even of Orthodox Christians. Neo-Donatists
go so far as to speak of the Church as deprived of grace or as being
"impure." The Church is being replaced by notions of a "Christian society" or "Christianity-in-general," which subvert the image of the Church as the source of the written Word of God. It is
as though the gates of hell were rising up against the Church,
seeking to separate her from Jesus Christ and impeding her task of
promoting salvation, a task entrusted to her by her Founder.

Alexander Khomiakov wrote, "the Church cannot teach
against her own dogma; she cannot teach against her own faith."[5]
We firmly believe that our Orthodox Church of today is the very
same Church that was founded by Jesus Christ and His apostles.
In the Church we preserve and proclaim basic beliefs and truths
of God's revelation that must never be replaced or deformed, de-
spite whatever pressures contemporary history may bring to bear.

The dogma of the Church is remembered and beautifully expressed in a morning prayer:

> First of all, remember, O Lord, your Holy Catholic and Apostolic
> Church, which you have purchased with your own blood. Protect and
> strengthen her, and grant her to grow upon the earth. Preserve your
> Church in purity, in peace and in safety, from the gates of hell, by the
> divine grace and power of the Holy Spirit.[6]

its fold is itself lapsed. Such a Church cannot possess the divine grace or true sacraments, including baptism. Thus, according to Donatists, the personal unworthiness
of a bishop was identified with the nature of the Church. Novatian held a rigorous
attitude toward re-admitting to the Church those members who had lapsed under
persecution. He was to become the first anti-pope, seceding in 251. For further
reading on the subject of these heresies, see: Vladimir Troitskii, *Ocherki iz istorii
dogmata o Tserkvi* (Moscow, 1913) 109, 110, 291-293, 480-490, 385.

5   A.S. Khomiakov, *The Church is One* (New York, 1979).
6   "The Morning Prayers," in *The Orthodox Prayer Book* (Wilkes-Barre, PA, 1934)
    44-46.

# 2

# The Divine Plan of Salvation

"And He put all things under His feet, and gave
Him to be head over all things to the church,
which is His body, the fullness of Him who fills all
in all" (Eph 1:22-23)

The salvation of mankind involves the restoration of unity between man and God, culminating in man's deification. It signifies the Christian's entrance into eternal life in the Kingdom of God, and it entails his spiritual perfection through a moral and spiritual ascent in holiness of life to the full stature of Jesus Christ.

Salvation of the soul is the most important task and goal in the life of every Orthodox Christian. It depends "on our Lord Jesus Christ granting to man the living power of divine grace with which Christians can defeat the power of the Devil. The grace of God is given for our salvation, but not without our personal, complete, and free cooperation in the spiritual perfection of our life."[1]

It was the pre-eternal design or plan of God the Father, initiated before the foundation of the world, to create an *economy of salvation*, and thereby to bless us in His Only-begotten Son, Jesus Christ. When the fullness of time arrived (Gal 4:4), the Word of God became incarnate (Jn 1:14). Being God's Word in human flesh, God's Son suffered, died on the Cross, was resurrected, and ascended into heaven, to sit at the right hand of God in glory (Phil 2:5-11). Christ then sent the Holy Spirit into the world, in order that through His apostles He might establish His Kingdom

---

1 Archimandrite Sergii (Stragorodskii), *Pravoslavnoie uchenie o spasenii* (Moscow, 1894), 140-141.

on earth in the form of the one, holy, catholic and apostolic Church (Jn 20:22; Acts 2:1-4). This Church is Christ's body, the possessor and repository of truth and the grace of God.

Those who enter the vineyard of God's Kingdom in Christ, God's holy Church, become participants in God's divine grace. They are purified and sanctified through the holy sacraments. Laboring spiritually by fulfilling the commandments of God until their last breath, they inherit eternal life in divine unity with Christ, who is enthroned at the right hand of God the Father in His Kingdom. This is the path of salvation established by God in His Holy Church.

Although the Church originated on earth at a specific time and in a certain place, the Church can trace her divine origin and foundation before time and the creation of the world, to the divine plan to conform fallen mankind to sonship in Christ through the Holy Spirit.

The meaning of the joyous mystery of the Divine Plan for the salvation of mankind is most eloquently expressed by St John of Damascus, who describes God's care and concern for fallen humanity:

> In Paradise, being ensnared by the temptation of the Devil, man broke the commandments of his Creator. As a consequence, man was stripped of God's grace, trust and confidence. Being condemned to toil and banished from Paradise, man became subject to corruption and death. Yet notwithstanding man's fallen state, God, the source of life and love, and who in His graciousness bestowed on man an eternal life of happiness, did not in His mercy abandon or disregard fallen man. For it was sin and corruption that brought ruin and death into human life.
>
> Now the Lord and Creator Himself undertook a struggle on behalf of His own creation, by becoming man's Savior through His divine works. And since the Devil ensnared man by promising that man would become god, he in turn was himself ensnared by the appearance of the divine Redeemer in the guise of flesh. In this action there was revealed at once the goodness, the wisdom, the justice and the power of God.
>
> God's goodness was revealed in that He did not disregard the frailty of His handiwork, but was moved with compassion for man in his fall,

and stretched forth His love to him. God's justice was revealed in that He saved man not by force, but by the most incomprehensible and seemingly impossible means, rescuing man "like by like" [i.e., assuming and glorifying fallen human nature through His Incarnation]. God's wisdom was seen in that God devised the most fitting solution for the salvation of mankind.

By the good pleasure of God the Father, the Only-begotten Son and Word of God, being of one essence with the Father and the Holy Spirit, bent the heavens and descended to earth. Remaining perfect God, He became perfect Man, thus manifesting the boundless might of God. Accordingly, the Incarnate Son of God, the God-Man Jesus Christ, being the Mediator between God and men, presents an ideal example of humility, without which there is no salvation.[2]

The origin and nature of the Church derive directly from our Lord and Savior Jesus Christ, the incarnate Son of God, whose coming into the world, in accordance with the Holy Scriptures, was predestined by God the Father even before the foundation of the world. It was included in God's pre-eternal council (plan or design) for the salvation of the world by "the precious blood of Christ, as of a lamb without blemish and without spot who verily was foreordained before the foundation of the world, but was manifested in these last times for your sake"(1 Pet 1:19-20). In this was revealed "the wisdom of God in a mystery, even the hidden wisdom which God ordained before the world unto our glory" (1 Cor 2:7). In Christ "God hath blessed us with all spiritual blessings in the heavenly places, even as He has chosen us before the foundation of the world, that we should be holy and without blemish before Him in love" (Eph 1:3-4). And this He has done "having predestined us unto the adoption of children by Jesus Christ to Himself, according to the good pleasure of His will, to the praise of the glory of His grace, wherein He hath made us accepted in the Beloved" (Eph 1:5-6). The mystery and purpose of God's will was to gather together into one, all things in

---

2  St John of Damascus, "Exposition of the Orthodox Faith," in *Polnoie sobranie tvorenii*, Book 3, 1 (St Petersburg, 1913).

heaven and on earth, in Christ, "in whom we have redemption through His blood, the forgiveness of sins, according to the riches of His grace" (Eph 1:7).[3]

Thus, the economy or divine plan of God reveals to the human race "what is the fellowship of the mystery, which from the beginning of the world has been hidden in God, who created all things by Jesus Christ; to the intent that now unto the principalities and powers in heavenly places might be known by the Church the manifold wisdom of God" (Eph 3:9-10). "Truly our fellowship (communion) is with the Father and with His Son Jesus Christ" (1 Jn 1:3), to make us "fellow citizens with the saints and members of the household of God" (Eph 2:19).

Therefore, our Lord Jesus Christ is called the "Alpha and the Omega," the "First and the Last," the "Beginning and the End" (Rev 1:8, 11, 17; 2:8; 22:13). In God's pre-eternal design He not only loved the world, but He preordained the entrance of the Son of God into the world, the incarnation of the Word of God: "For God so loved the world that He gave His Only-begotten Son, that whosoever believeth in Him should not perish but have everlasting life...[and] that the world through Him might be saved" (Jn 3:16-17).

God is love. He manifested His love when He sent His Only-begotten Son into the world, that we might live through Him—be saved by Him, for "He is the propitiation for our sins" (1 Jn 4:8-10). God predestined us "to be conformed to the image of His Son...for He did not spare His own Son, but delivered Him for us all" (Rom 8:29, 32). Thereby, in Christ we become a "people of God...a chosen generation, a royal priesthood, a holy nation, a peculiar people," that we "should show forth the praises of

3  Redemption is essentially freedom from slavery: Christ redeemed us from our sins (Eph 1:7; Col 1:14); He gave His life as a ransom for many (Mt 20:28; Mk 10:45); He is a propitiation through faith in His blood (Rom 3:25); by His own blood He obtained an eternal redemption for us (Heb 9:12); He bought us at a price (1 Cor 6:20).

Him who hath called [us] out of darkness into His marvelous light" (1 Pt 2:9-10).

God the Father originated the redeeming plan—the time, the manner of execution, and the goal which was entrusted to His Son, who Himself is the Mediator between God and man: "When the fullness of the time had come, God sent forth His Son, born of a woman, born under the law, to redeem them that were under the law, that we might receive the adoption as sons" (Gal 4:4-5).

St Theophan the Recluse, commenting on God's Divine Plan of salvation, answered this question: "What did God promise when He blessed us with all spiritual blessing in the heavenly places in Christ?"

> Nothing material or earthly, but spiritual and eternal. All spiritual gifts are given to man in Christ, by Christ, and because of Christ. The reverse is also true: through Christ as the Intermediary, all our blessings and adoration must ascend to God. As God through and in Christ blesses us and grants us all spiritual gifts, so we also through, in and with Christ must give glory to God, who blesses us from heaven. As God does nothing in our regard without Christ, so nothing reaches God from us, if it is not through Christ.[4]

It is evident that our Lord Jesus Christ is the center, the source, and the giver of all divine gifts and of all divine life, to all members of His Church. Therefore our life must be Christ-centered, since we are chosen by God to be, in Christ, "holy and undefiled" and the "children of God" (Eph 1:4-6). Sonship and holiness are inseparable. "For as many as received Him, to them He gave power to become children of God" (Jn 1:12). Sonship is not a nominal act; it is a new birth from God (Jn 1:13). Thereby all of God's children can address Him, "*Abba*, Father," since they are conformed to the image of His Son (Rom 8:14, 15, 29).

---

4 St Theophan, "Commentary on the Epistle to the Ephesians," in *Tolkovanie: poslaniia sv. apostola Pavla: k Efeseiam* (Moscow, 1893), 50 [*In Bibliography, see* Feofan, Saint, Bishop of Tambov and Shatsk].

Why are we worthy to become children of God? Because in Christ we have redemption through His blood and the forgiveness of sins (Eph 1:7). Thus redemption may be understood as the divine action which *objectively* embraces the whole world, whereas the forgiveness of sins resulting from the redemption is *subjectively* applied to every believer in Christ. Once shed on the Cross, the redeeming blood of Jesus Christ mediates eternally between God and man (Heb 9:15). On earth the redeeming work of Christ is continued by His Church.

To God alone belongs the glory and the initiative of the world's salvation. He blessed us with the heavenly blessing, chose and predestined us to be holy and undefiled, elected us to be redeemed and saved by His beloved Son, and granted to us divine sonship, in order that by Christ, with Christ, and in Christ, we may attain union with God in love, life, and holiness.

St Theophan explains the mystery of God's will and His eternal purpose in Christ our Lord, known by the Church as the manifold wisdom of God (Eph 3:9-11):

> [This mystery is God's] highly exalted human nature in the Person of our Savior, yet did not separate Him from us at the throne of God, but gave Christ to be the Head of the Church, which is His Body. And if the honor of the Head is reflected in the Body, then the exaltation and glory of the Head means the elevation of the Body as well. That means the elevation of all of us who believe and who constitute the living unity of the Body of Christ, His Holy Church.[5]

According to the divine plan, redemption became reality when the Son of God, who eternally dwells with the Father, "took the form of a servant and was made in the likeness of men...He humbled Himself and became obedient unto death, even the death of the Cross" (Phil 2:7-8). "The Word was made flesh and dwelt among us" (Jn 1:14). Indeed, "great is the mystery of godliness: God was manifest in the flesh, justified in the Spirit, seen of An-

5   Ibid, 122.

gels, preached unto Gentiles, believed on in the world, received up into glory" (1 Tim 3:16).

Divine Life entered into the world: "I am the life...In Him was life, and the life was the light of men...I come that they might have life and have it more abundantly"(Jn 14:6; 1:4; 10:10). The Son of God, Jesus Christ, assumed into His divine person perfect human nature, thus bringing divine and eternal life into the world. This is His wonderful incarnation—and so we believe and confess that the Son of God, for our salvation, was incarnate of the Holy Spirit and the Virgin Mary and became man, thus opening for us the possibility to live in Him (Gal 2:20). This is the goal of every Orthodox Christian who hopes to partake in God's precious gift for every human being to become a participant of His divine nature (2 Pet 1:4).

New life is received when we are grafted onto Christ in the sacrament of baptism. In Christ, by Christ, and with Christ, we are united to God as members of His divine Body, the Church (Eph 1:23).

In conclusion, we can affirm that the mystery of the world's salvation was included in the design conceived by God the Father from all eternity, before the foundation of the world. To God belong the glory and the initiative of salvation. He blessed us with the heavenly blessing, chose and predestined us to be holy and undefiled, elected us to be redeemed and saved by His beloved Son, and granted us sonship in order that by Christ, with Christ, and in Christ we may attain union with God in love, life and holiness in His Church.

In Christ, "who is the image of the invisible God, the firstborn of every creature" (Col 1:15), God revealed Himself to mankind. He did so, in order to heal fallen human nature without destroying its freedom; to completely renew and regenerate fallen man by uniting him with God in divine life and love; and to restore man's immortality, destroyed by sin, by resurrecting him into the divine life of the Holy Trinity. "You are the temple of the living God; as God hath said: 'I will dwell with them and walk with them, and they shall be my people... And I will be a Father unto you, and you shall be my sons and daughters,' said the Lord Almighty" (2 Cor 6:16, 18). In the incarnate Son of God this promise of God the Father was fulfilled.

# 3

# The Holy Trinity: Source of Theanthropic Life

*"I pray not for the world, but for them which
Thou has given Me, for they are Thine...
Whom Thou has given Me, that they may be one,
as we are" (Jn 17:9, 11)*

God is the one and only source and giver of Life. God is Life itself. He brought all of creation into existence from nonexistence. He called Adam to life by the "breath of life," making him a "living being" (Gen 2:7). Mankind strives ceaselessly to attain this life, for "God did not create death; He created all things that they might have life" (Wis 2:23). Eve, therefore, became "the mother of all living" (Gen 3:20).[1]

Indeed, God the Father is the source of life and *Life* itself: "I am Being (I AM THAT I AM)...thus say to the children of Israel, I AM hath sent me to you" (Ex 3:14). "I am the Alpha and the Omega, who is and who was and who is to come, the Almighty" (Rev 1:8).

God gives life to all things (1 Tim 6:13). "God has given us eternal life, and this life is in His Son... He that has the Son has life" (1 Jn 5:11-12). God the Father is the ultimate source of His divine Son and Word, and the Holy Spirit, "for from Him and through Him and to Him are all things" (Rom 11:36). God the

---

1   What is the origin of evil? "By the envy of the Devil, death entered the world, and all who are in his possession experience it" (Wis 2:24). "Sin is lawlessness" (1 Jn 3:4) and rejection of the will of God (Rom 5:17-19). The Devil was the first to sin (1 Jn 3:8; cf. Rom 5:12).

Father is the Living God (Mt 16:16). He has "Life in Himself"
(Jn 5:26). From Him all fatherhood on earth and in heaven gets
its name (Eph 3:15). The work of Jesus Christ is to the glory of
God the Father (Phil 2:11). Love is a way of life, for "he who does
not love does not know God, for God is love" (1 Jn 4:8).

The Son of God, Jesus Christ, is the true Life which He pos-
sesses in Himself (Jn 1:4). Eternal life is to know the one, true
God, and Jesus Christ whom He has sent (Jn 17:3), who is the
Son of the Living God (Mt 16:16). Jesus Christ is the "Way, the
Truth and the Life" (Jn 14:6). He has the "words of eternal life"
(Jn 6:68). He is the "Living Water," and the water He gives leads
us into everlasting Life (Jn 4:10, 14). "Our hands have handled the
Word of Life...for the Life was manifested and we have seen it... the
eternal Life which was with the Father and was manifested to us"
(1 Jn 1:1, 2). He is the "Resurrection and the Life" (Jn 11:25), "a
life-giving Spirit" (1 Cor 15:45).

The hope of all Christians is that Christ should live in them, as
he lived in the Apostle Paul (Gal 2:19). With Christ we are walk-
ing "in a newness of life" (Rom 6:4). If we die with Christ, we
shall also "live with Him" (Rom 6:8). Being dead unto sin, we are
"alive unto God through Jesus Christ our Lord" (Rom 6:11). The
wages of sin are death, but the free gift of God is "eternal life
through Jesus Christ our Lord" (Rom 6:23). In Him are the
words of life (Acts 5:20). We shall be saved by His life (Rom
5:10). The "divine power" of Jesus Christ "has granted to us all
things that pertain to life and godliness" (2 Pet 1:3). These gifts of
eternal life—with divine love, fullness, and unity—are granted
through Jesus Christ to the Church: "I appoint for you a Kingdom as my Father appointed it to me, that you may sit and drink
at the table in my Kingdom" (Lk 22:29).

Through the Holy Spirit Christians receive new life; they become "a new creation" and "children of God" (Jn 3:1-13; Acts
8:14-25; Rom 8:14-16), thereby also becoming the "temple of

God" (Eph 2:20-22). The Holy Spirit is the "power of the Most High" (Lk 1:35). The Spirit of the Son is sent into our hearts by God, making of us "sons of God" who cry, "*Abba*, Father!" (Gal 4:6). "Know you not that you are the temples of God, and that the Spirit of God dwelleth in you? For the Temple of God is holy, which temple you are" (1 Cor 3:16-17). And again: "you are the temple of the living God" (2 Cor 6:16). By the Holy Spirit we possess the love of God, and through our Lord Jesus Christ we have joy in God (Rom 5:5, 11).

According to St Epiphanius, the work of Christ and the Holy Spirit are one:

> Jesus Christ is sent by the Father, and the Holy Spirit is also sent; Jesus Christ speaks in the saints, the Holy Spirit speaks also. Christ heals, and the Holy Spirit likewise heals. Christ sanctifies, and so does the Holy Spirit. In fact grace, filial adoption, good works, salvation, eternal glory, in other words, all the manifestations of divine life are referred to Christ and to the Holy Spirit alike.[2]

"God the Father is the source and the origin of Life. The Son of God can be defined as the essence of Life. In Him was revealed the true meaning of divine Life. The Holy Spirit is the Power of Life or the Breath of Life."[3]

The incarnation of the Word of God is the revelation of God's love entering the world. The incarnation is the source and foundation of divine life within the Church, whose purpose is "to give eternal life to as many as Thou hast given me." "This is eternal life, that they might know you" (Jn 17:2-3; cf. 1 Jn 5:13). "He who has the Son has life, and he who has not the Son of God does not have life" (1 Jn 5:12). Because the Son came into the world, we have life through Him (1 Jn 4:9). Because of His great love for us, God made His Son "the propitiation for our sins" (1 Jn 4:10, 12). Our unity with Christ, therefore, must be a living, organic unity: "I am the vine, you are the branches" (Jn 15:4-6); and He

---

2   F. Prat, *Theology of St Paul*, vol. 2 (Westminster, 1961), 291-292.
3   S.S. Verhovskoy, *Bog i chelovek* (New York, 1953), 272.

promises that He will be with His Church "until the end of the world" (Mt 28:20).

*On the Incarnation,* the classic work of St Athanasius the Great of Alexandria, will forever be of great significance to Orthodox Christians for explaining the essence of Christianity by pointing toward the goal of Christian life. Let us consider a few of the messages St Athanasius presents.

Through the incarnation, the abyss that separated man from God, the creature from the Creator, was once and for all closed by the coming of Christ the Word. In Him man has received the possibility to participate in the divine life and to attain deification (2 Pet 1:4). This constitutes his salvation, which is the goal of human life. In this saving act lies the essence of Christianity, and it is realized precisely within the Church.

The Word assumed human nature in order to deify mankind. He overcame death not only for Himself, but for all of us: "by the grace of the resurrection, banishing death from them like straw consumed by the fire."[4] Being by nature God, the Word was united with all mankind by assuming human nature, and by reason of His one Body He came to dwell among men. St Athanasius declares that, "the Word was made man, that we might be made god."[5]

St Athanasius' teaching on the incarnation was taken up and developed by St Cyril of Alexandria, who explained the mystery of the unity of the incarnate Son of God with His Body, the Church.

---

4  St Athanasius, "On the Incarnation," in *A Select Library of Nicene and Post-Nicene Fathers of the Christian Church* (Grand Rapids, 1957), chapter 8.

5  Ibid., chapter 54. The idea that "God made Himself man, that man might become god" was already expressed by St Irenaeus, but with St Athanasius, the idea of *theosis* or divinization became, as one theologian expressed it, the "religious ideal of Orthodoxy." The idea of *theosis* is accepted by many different aspects of Orthodox mystical theology and spirituality, and it became foundational for understanding the Eucharist.

According to St Cyril, through the Incarnation of the Son of God, our Savior Jesus Christ, humanity and divinity—the flesh and the eternal Word—are united without change occurring in either nature. Jesus of Nazareth is one with the Word—the God-Man: one Person in two natures, who is and who offers us true, incorruptible and eternal life. Upon assuming full human nature, Christ unites our human nature and His divine nature, thereby bestowing on us creatures the possibility of eternal life.

In the eucharistic experience of the Church we become communicants of life eternal, since we are *contained in* Christ and vivified by Him. We constitute the Body of Christ by being incorporated into Him. Once He unites human nature to Himself, that nature becomes fully life-giving, since it is united with the eternal, divine Word. Christ's humanity becomes the Body of Life itself, in whom the fullness of God dwells corporally (Col 2:9). The Word makes His Body, the Church, a life-giving Body, since He conveys His own power and life to it. How is this done? St Cyril answers: "We can neither fully understand nor clearly explain. We must venerate the mystery in silence, and in faith that passes understanding." Christ's Body is life-giving because it is the temple of the Word, the Church of the living God. Thus, according to St Cyril, Christ in His humanity assumes our infirmities and our death, in order that we may receive eternal life by being united to the life-giving Word. Since Christ *is* Life, He has made His humanity absolutely universal and life-giving. He is the life of men, the mediator, and head of His Body, the Church.[6]

St Cyril pursues this theme in his reflections on the Holy Trinity. Our return to God the Father, he writes, is effected through our Savior Jesus Christ, but only through the participation and sanctifying work of the Holy Spirit, who elevates us to the Son and thereby unites us to the Father. In the Holy Spirit we become

6  St Cyril, "Commentary on the Gospel of John," in *The Whole Christ*, E. Mersch (Milwaukee, 1938), 337-364 [English Text].

sharers and partakers of the divine nature.[7] Moreover, the manner
of the divine unity (Jn 17:21), with the identity of essence shared
by the Persons of the Holy Trinity, is to be mirrored or reflected
in the unity of the faithful. This occurs through their mutual harmony and concord, as it does by the unity of nature by which
God's human creatures are joined to one another and united to
God in Christ, who assumed our human nature in order that we
might share in His divine nature.[8]

St Cyril's teaching on the Eucharist is most realistic, revealing,
and beautiful. The Holy Eucharist is the center of unity between
God and man. It is the sacrament of communion with Christ
through His Body and Blood. In the Eucharist the three persons
of the Holy Trinity work together to accomplish our salvation:

> Christ comes to us corporally as Man, uniting Himself with us through
> the mystery of the Eucharist. But as God He comes spiritually by the
> power and love of the Holy Spirit, who enters into us, to infuse a new
> life in us and to make us partakers of His divine nature. Thus we see that
> the bond of our union with God the Father is Christ in the Holy Spirit.
> We are perfected in union with God the Father through our mediator
> Jesus Christ in the Holy Spirit. For when we receive within us corpo-
> rally and spiritually the true Son who is essentially united with the Fa-
> ther, we have the glory of participating and communicating in the di-
> vine nature.[9]

In the Eucharist, the Church proclaims the death of the
Only-begotten Son of God and announces His resurrection and
ascension to heaven. We who partake of the consecrated gifts are
sanctified by the precious Body and Blood of Christ, and thereby
we come to enjoy a divine indwelling of Christ in ourselves. For
being God, He embodies life in His very nature; and when He becomes one with mankind by assuming human nature, He bestows
life upon us. In the Eucharist God Himself infuses the power of
life into the bread and wine, changing them into His own Body

7   Ibid., 353.
8   H.S. Bettenson, (comp.), *The Latter Christian Fathers* (London, 1970), 266.
9   E. Mersch, *The Whole Christ* (Milwaukee, 1938), 348.

and Blood so that we may receive them as the source of life. Thus the Body of life within us proves to be a "life-giving seed."[10]

St Cyril speaks of the similarity between the Incarnation and the Eucharist. Just as the incarnate Word—Life itself—by uniting Himself with human nature, elevated it to His own image and made it capable of imparting life, so also in the Eucharist Christ enters into us, transforms us into His own image, and gives us life eternal. Just as that Body which the Word made His own is life-giving, so we who partake in His sacred Body and Blood are wholly vivified. For the Word abides in us, both divinely by the Holy Spirit, and humanly by His sacred Body and precious Blood. The Body of Christ within us binds us into unity, for that Body is never divided.[11]

Therefore we believe:

[t]hat the Word of God, by uniting Himself in an ineffable and mysterious union with a body born of the Virgin, has made the Body life-giving, since the Word, being God, is Life itself. His purpose was to make us partake of Himself in a manner both spiritual and material, to make us victorious over corruption and to destroy the law of sin that reigned in our members."[12]

Jesus Christ is God and Man in one Person. Through His Body, which is His Church, He blesses those who believe in Him and makes them co-corporal with Himself and with one another. They are thus bound together into unity with Christ by means of His one holy Body, the Church. For this reason the Church is called the Body of Christ, and we separately His members (Eph 1:23; 1 Cor 12:27). Since we are united with the one Christ through His sacred Body, we belong no more to ourselves, but to Christ.[13]

The one God is true divine life, and by keeping God's commandments we can enter into eternal life (Mt 19:17). For "by the

---

10 Bettenson, *The Latter Christian Fathers*, 268.
11 Mersch, *The Whole Christ*, 344.
12 Ibid., 344-345.
13 Ibid., 346; cf. "St Hilary" and 304.

righteousness of one [man] there came upon all men the justification [that leads] to life" (Rom 5:18). God is the source of life and
of the existence of all things. To strive toward the image and likeness of God is the highest and most wonderful goal of every
Christian, to be perfect, even as our Father is perfect (Mt 5:48).
"For we are His workmanship, created in Christ Jesus unto good
works" (Eph 2:10).

Thus, Jesus Christ is the way to the truth and to eternal life: "I
am the vine, you are the branches" (Jn 15:6). This means that the
Church is one, holy, catholic and apostolic because the Lord is
one and holy. As our Lord is the Way, the Truth and the Life (Jn
14:6), so also is the Church; for the Church is one with Christ:
body of His Body (cf. Eph 5:30). She is bonded to Him as the
branch is grafted onto a living vine. The Church is growing in
Him and constantly nourished by Him. The Church must never
be imagined as separate from Jesus Christ, or from the Father or
the Holy Spirit.[14]

Man's desire for true life is fulfilled for those who believe in Jesus
Christ. In Him human persons inherit eternal life, for those who
live in God do not die (Jn 3:36; 6:40, 47). Divine in its origin, the
Church as the divine life of the Holy Trinity given to believers is
destined to live and act on earth according to worldly conditions.
The Church is powerful, for she is founded on the divine love,
power and will of God the Father, who desires our salvation in Jesus Christ. Everything that comes directly from the divine source
of the Holy Trinity and is received by the Church, is holy, pure,
and undefiled. These qualities belong to the true nature of the
Church. This divine life of the Holy Trinity, this divine presence
and power, now dwells within the Church in a living unity with
the human element, creating divine-human life.

Divine life and divine grace, which sanctify the Church, constitute her perfect divine nature. Human actions within the

14  See St John of Kronstadt, *Moia zhisn' vo Khriste,* vol. 2 (Paris, 1984), 234.

Church, even those performed in the name of the Church, are nevertheless often far from being perfect. They often reveal human weaknesses and sin. For this reason it is important for any Orthodox Christian not to identify human iniquity and human sinfulness with the theanthropic being of the Church.

Believers in Jesus Christ become participants of true life, since that life dwells mystically in their souls as the Kingdom of God (Lk 17:21). Those who seek true life can find it only in God, as our Lord declares: "He that believeth in me has eternal life" (Jn 6:47). That divine life is revealed in the Church together with the means of achieving it.

St Cyprian of Carthage affirmed: "No one can have God as Father who does not have the Church as Mother."[15] God gave His servants to the Church so that they might achieve eternal life (Eph 4:11-12).

The "fullness of time" is the time of the divine incarnation and redemption, the beginning of the coming of new and true life into the world. This divine, true life was fully revealed in the Church. For the Church united all those who are in one Lord, one faith, one baptism, and one God and Father of all. Thereby, the one Christian Church is composed of "one Body, one Spirit" (Eph 4:4). Just as we cannot think of our Lord Jesus Christ as the Redeemer apart from the true life that flows from Him, so we cannot think of Christianity apart from the Church, which bears this divine life.

In the Gospel of St John, the oneness of the Church is likened by our Lord to the oneness of the Father and the Son in the Holy Spirit, the oneness of the Holy Trinity itself: "You are in me and I in you, so they may be one in us." "Father, keep those whom Thou hast given me, that they may be one as we are one" (Jn 17:21, 24).

The essence of this unity of mankind in the Holy Trinity, the main principle of life in the Church, is love—love, which our

---

15  St Cyprian of Carthage, in *Patrology*, J. Quasten, vol. 2 (Westminster, 1949), 351.

Lord Jesus Christ, in His prayer to the Father, established as the very foundation of the Church (Jn 17:26). Christ commanded His Apostles to live in such a unity of love (Jn 13:34-35; 15:12-17). This principle of love is fundamental to the essence of the Church, for "God is love" (1 Jn 4:8). Therefore the Church grounds its love in Christ, for Jesus Christ, the God-Man, loved His Church as He loved His own Body: Christ loved the Church and gave Himself for her; Christ loves, nourishes and cherishes the Church (Eph 5:25, 29). Therefore, A.S. Khomiakov declared: "Love is the crown and glory of the Church."[16]

Accordingly, Christ calls His Church to a response of love: "Thou shalt love the Lord thy God with all thy heart, and with all thy soul, and with all thy mind, and with all thy strength," since those who love their neighbor are not far from the Kingdom of God (Mt 22:37-40; Mk 12:30-34).

Nevertheless, as our Lord affirms, "Without Me you can do nothing"(Jn 15:5). Therefore, in order for the faithful to live in Christ and in His Church, it is necessary for them to be reborn, that is, to be regenerated into new life: "Except a man be born again, he cannot see the Kingdom of God" (Jn 3:3, 5). New life in the incarnate Son of God, our Savior Jesus Christ, opens the way for the believer to enter Christ's Kingdom, His Church:

> In the Person of Jesus Christ humanity became a participant in the divine nature, and without the Incarnation of the Son of God, it would have been impossible to unite people to the Church. Thus the incarnate Son of God—the God-Man Jesus Christ—is the foundation of the Church on earth.[17]

The Church as the Body of Christ participates in the divine life of the Holy Trinity. The Church is one, and all who participate in the life of the Church are united one to another in God. For God is one, and one is Christ the Lord, and one is the Holy

16  A.S. Khomiakov, *The Church is One* (New York, 1979), paragraph, 109.
17  Archimandrite Illarion (Troitskii), *Khristianstva net bez Tserkvi* (São Paulo, 1954), 4.

Spirit, and so too one is the Church as the possessor and bearer of God's life.

Fr. Sergius Bulgakov continues this reflection regarding the divine-human quality of the Church:

> The idea that the Church is the Body of Christ—who in turn is the God-Man, true God and true Man—evokes the thought that the Body of the Incarnate Christ is the Church, and that in the Church humanity is deified, since members of the Church truly participate in His divine life.[18]

Likewise St Theophan declares:

> The whole of humanity, united with its divine source in Christ, is the living Body of the Incarnate Word of God, historically revealed as the God-Man, our Savior Jesus Christ. This living Body of Christ is the Church, which already possesses all necessary means for attaining the future peaceful and perfect life."[19]

God Himself continually supports the supernatural life of regenerated humanity, the life of the Church, since it is theanthropic life in the Holy Trinity. In order for a person to enter into the Kingdom of God, the Church, one must first be born again of water and the Holy Spirit (Jn 3:5-7). Thus the Church can initially be defined as the unity of human life in the divine life of the Holy Trinity, the life of all newly born believers in Christ, the Son of the living God. The Holy Scriptures present the Church as a local community or as the sum of local communities, all of which are united by the one and the same divine life. The one universal Church of Christ possesses the fullness of divine life, in which all who are united to Christ participate.

The Church is composed of two elements or, we may even dare to say, two natures. One is divine and eternal life, which represents the inner essence, or nature, of the Church's being—her love, unity, and holiness. The other is the Church's human form

---

18 Archpriest S.N. Bulgakov, *Nevesta Agntsa* (Paris, 1945), 281.
19 St Theophan [Feofan], "Commentary on the Epistle to the Ephesians," in *Tolkovanie: poslaniia sv. apostola Pavla: k Efeseiam* (Moscow, 1893), 123, 124.

consisting of life in this world and the life of all those who have departed "this life" as members of the Church of Christ. The human element in the Church is visible and includes the holy sacraments, the hierarchy, Church structures, the Holy Scriptures and Holy Tradition.

> The main quality of the Church is that under the external forms of life there exists divine grace as the acting power of God. The Church is thus this divine life of grace both in this world and in the world beyond. She is the unending, permanent deification of man and the world itself. The most significant aspect of the life of the Church is this undivided unity between the external forms of the Church and her divine content."[20]

Sacraments, since they possess divine as well as material elements, exemplify this "undivided unity." And the Church herself leads both a transcendent and imminent, a heavenly and earthly, existence.

Such unity between the divine and human aspects of the Church's life is a mystery beyond all understanding. Thus the life of the Church herself is a mystery of faith, one that is revealed or opened only to the living experience of its members. This is why we believe in one, holy, catholic and apostolic Church.

Again, in Sergius Bulgakov's words:

> The Church is the unity of action between the Holy Spirit and her human members. The Church in its essence, as the unity of divine-human life, belongs to the realm of Divinity; the Church is from God. As a God-founded society, the Church exists within human history as Christ's Kingdom *within* this world but not *of* this world (Jn 18:37). The life of the Church is perceived by faith as a unique life, patterned after the oneness of the life of the Holy Trinity. The Church is one as well as holy, because of the fundamental presence in her life of the Holy Trinity. She is holy, undefiled, and cannot err, since her essence is hidden in God. She unites the eternal and the temporal, the uncreated and the created, in her sacraments, her hierarchy, and in the Word of God. The divine, invisible life of Jesus Christ is invisibly united with His con-

---

20 Archpriest S.N. Bulgakov, "*Ocherki ucheniia o Tserkvi*," in *Put'*, no. 1 (Paris, 1925), 55.

crete humanity, thus creating a bridge between heaven and earth, uniting in the Church the eternal God with His creation. The Church is the Incarnation of our Savior Jesus Christ, existing in the world until the end of the world. The Church is the locus of the Holy Spirit, who descended on the day of Pentecost to animate the Church. Thus the Church is the revelation of the Holy Trinity within the world.[21]

It can be said that the Church is the ladder from earth to heaven, by whose rungs God descends to earth and human persons ascend to heaven. Although she is of divine nature, by the will of God, the Church nevertheless necessarily possesses human and earthly forms of life, in the experience of all those who have accepted new life in the community of believers, in Christ, and in His Church.

According to St Theophan, the Recluse:

The Church of Christ, the Heavenly Jerusalem, the Mother of us all (Gal 4:26; Heb 12:22), lives on earth. However,

–The Church is called heavenly because of her heavenly foundation;

–The Church is called heavenly because the heavenly powers are acting in her;

–The Church is heavenly because of her closeness to heaven, with which she is united in perfect wholeness;

–The Church is heavenly because her goals of existence are heavenly;

–The Church is heavenly because she is filled with heavenly elements; (cf. Gal 4:26)

–The Church is heavenly because as Mother of us all, she gives birth to us, then prepares us to become citizens of the Heavenly Kingdom.[22]

Although the Church is the Heavenly Jerusalem, she is nevertheless an earthly, historical reality which mystically contains in herself heavenly, divine powers that manifest themselves in the holy sacraments, the hierarchy, divine services, the divine Word of God, and in the gifts of the Holy Spirit: faith, hope and love. This

21  Ibid., 55.
22  St Theophan [Feofan], "Commentary on the Epistle to the Galatians," in *Tolkovanie: poslaniia sv. apostola Pavla: k Galatam* (Moscow, 1893), 343.

is possible because the character of the divine sacraments is such that the power or grace of God is intrinsic to them, hidden and revealed in visible, material forms. The invisible divine nature of the sacraments is manifested by visible earthly realities (bread, wine, oil, and water).

> The Church in its nature exists on the border between present, earthly reality and future, heavenly reality. The Church is the Way into the Kingdom of God, just as the Church is the Kingdom of God in its earthly aspect. In the Church, the temporal is united with the eternal. The Church is the Body of Christ, already existing in glory, in eternity, at the throne of God. In her cosmic fullness she embraces the heavenly powers (Eph 1:20-23). But this does not exclude the fact that the same Body of Christ continues to grow in its fullness (Eph 4:11-16).[23]

We can distinguish these two elements, divine and human, by analyzing the names of the Church as they are given in the Holy Scriptures. These names demonstrate that the divine being of the Church is united with human, earthly elements: The Body of Christ, animated by the Holy Spirit; the Bride of Christ; the House or Household of God; the House of the Holy Spirit; the Temple of the Living God; the Assembly of God; the New Israel; the Heavenly Jerusalem; the Church of Christ. In all these names attributed to the Church we can see the perfect unity of the two elements, divine and human. In fact, the word *ekklesia*, the *Qehal Yahweh*, means "the People of God" or "the Assembly of God," which expresses the union of God with man. The term *ekklesia* contains in itself an important element of "visibility."[24] The fact that our Lord Jesus Christ called His society of believers the *ekklesia* has special significance for apologetics with those who believe the Church to be essentially invisible. The expression *ekklesia* implies a fundamental aspect of *visibility*, since in it there participate both spiritual realities and physical, human elements.

23 Bishop Kassian Bezobrazov, *Khristos i pervoe khristianskoe pokolenie* (Paris, 1950), 271-278.
24 V.V. Bolotov, *Lektsii po istorii drevnei Tserkvi*, vol. 1 (St Petersburg, 1907), 9-14.

Jesus Christ taught about the Kingdom of God. Yet on earth He founded His Church, whose members are "fellow citizens with the saints and members of the household of God" (Eph 2:19) called to be "a holy nation" (1 Pet 2:9).

As every Christian is led to strive for salvation by the Holy Trinity, so also in the Church the Holy Trinity lives and acts as a single divine life. There the divine power of God is present, acting within the Church and animating it. There, too, the divine Founder and Head of the Church, our Lord Jesus Christ, sanctifies with the seal of the Holy Spirit all who are baptized in the Name of the Holy Trinity when they enter into His Body (cf. Mt 28:19).

Thus, the Church is new life in God, in Christ and in the Holy Spirit. In Christ, divine life is united with humanity, and thus, theanthropic life becomes the inheritance of those who are baptized into Christ, accepting Him as the Son of the living God in the Holy Spirit.

In the incarnate Word, Jesus Christ, two perfect natures—divine and human—are perfectly united inseparably and without confusion. Christ the incarnate Son assumes perfect human nature. Thereby His Body, the Church, is united to Him in a bond of divine life and subordinated to Him in the Holy Spirit. The Church simultaneously possesses the divine life of Jesus Christ, and the love, life, and power of the Holy Trinity. It may even be said that the Church is theanthropic life in the Holy Trinity.

The Church as the Body of Christ, as deified humanity, had its beginning at the time of the incarnation of the Son of God. God assumed human nature, and human nature became divine in the person of Jesus Christ, the God-Man. Yet the act of assuming humanity into the Body of Christ is not accomplished by the incarnation or the resurrection alone. Jesus declares to His disciples: "It is better for you that I go to my Father" (Jn 16:7). The full realization of the Church on earth required the descent of the Holy Spirit at Pentecost, the day of the founding of the Church in time and space. Through the descent of the Holy Spirit, the Church became a participant in the divine life of the Holy Trinity. She began to lead a most blessed life in the Holy Spirit, whereby the Spirit animates the Church and her members.

In the Church there is unity of life between Christ and ourselves. We are in Him as He is in the Father, and as the Father and Son are in us (Jn 14:20; 17:21). We become an extension or prolongation of Him, as the body united with the head, the branches to the vine, and the bride to the bridegroom. We form with Him one living organism, animated by one divine life. This life originates with the Father and passes to His Son, the incarnate Word, who in turn is united to human nature, in order that He might embrace the whole human race as its Savior and Redeemer. Because Christ is the God-Man, in Him and by Him, His mystical Body, the Church, possesses a theanthropic existence. Members of the Church share fully in the theanthropic life of the Holy Trinity, and they do so through our Lord Jesus Christ. For the Church is the realization and continuation of Christ's redeeming work on behalf of all mankind.

Jesus Christ receives life from the Father and makes it flow into us through our participation in Him. Thereby He enables us to live in true unity with the Holy Spirit, and in unity with one another through the visible institution of the Church's sacraments. Our Lord Jesus Christ is the Way, the Truth and the Life (Jn 14:6). The Church as the fullness of Christ is also the Way, the Truth and the Life; for she is wholly united to Christ, she lives by His life. "In the apostolic hierarchy, Jesus Christ is present in the Church as the Way. In the *Symbol of Faith* He is present as the Truth. In the Holy Sacraments He is present in the Church as the Life."[25]

Thus, in the Church all that is divine, eternal and unchangeable—life, love, truth and oneness—expresses the basic essence of the Church. "The Word became flesh" (Jn 1:14). Because of this

---

25  V. Soloviov, *Dukhovnye osnovy zhizni* (New York, 1958), 108.

miracle, the deified Body of Christ permanently lives in the world in the form of the Church. Sharing the one life of the Church, we can strive to be perfect as God the Father is perfect, that we might inherit eternal blessedness and salvation in the Kingdom of God.

Eternal life, love, and unity from God the Father, through the Son, and by the Holy Spirit unite all those who are "in Christ," that they might be one with Him. The divine mystery of love is at the very heart of the unity of life (Jn 17:11, 23-26), since Jesus Christ Himself gives a new commandment of love to His apostles (Jn 13:34-35; 1 Jn 3:14).

Within the Church we all are one in the unity of the three Persons of the Holy Trinity. To understand the unity of the Church, it is necessary to know the mystery of the Holy Trinity. The life of the Church is centered on the Second Person of the Trinity, on Christ the Savior, since His mission is "to gather together into one the children of God" (Jn 11:52). In fact, Christ's own qualities are passed on to His Church: His love and life, His knowledge and peaceful joy, with the power of His resurrection and ascension. Believing in Christ, we are incorporated through the sacraments and our spiritual life into His Body as members of His Church, and there we strive toward restoration of the "image and likeness of God" (Gn 1:27).

Commenting on Ephesians 3:16, St Theophan, the Recluse has shown us the road toward achieving this goal:

> Creating human nature by means distinguished from other acts of creation, God breathed into man the breath of His divine life. This breath of God in human nature is the highest spiritual aspect, by which the intellectual consciousness of man, enlightened by the fear of God, constantly strives toward still higher spiritual states. For it is the natural desire of the human spirit to ascend toward the source of its existence, offering itself, with all its talents and possessions, to God.

> For this reason a man is endowed with the authority and power of grace to overcome his human desires, weaknesses and corrupting passions. Now living in God's grace, power and strength, man's life includes the

soul, with all its intellectual and scientific knowledge, embracing a whole multitude of spiritual gifts, together with the physical and material aspects of life, so that all might be spiritualized by the grace of God.

When such an effort and experience become part of normal human existence, then man truly realizes in himself the 'image and likeness' of God intended for him. Yet it is evident that such an ideal state can only be achieved with the help of God, to whom man completely dedicates himself, and in whom man finds the goal and meaning of his life.[26]

Such a state can only be attained through our Savior Jesus Christ. He is in the Father, we are in Him and He in us, so that our minds can be set on heavenly rather than on earthly things (Col 3:2).

The Church, in the most profound sense, is the realization of the Kingdom of God on earth. She is Christ's Kingdom of divine grace, life, love, and divine unity, in which the faithful believers receive sanctifying grace, new life, and salvation in God's eternal Kingdom. Thus the Church is not simply "a society of those who believe in Christ." She is rather the divinely founded institution in which Christ dwells in those who believe in Him, and in which He grants His boundless gifts to them. The Church, as the divine institution of sanctification, education, enlightenment, and protection, is truly our Mother.

The unity of the Church with Christ is living, full and organic. It is the unity of the people with Christ, joined to Him as the body to the head, or the branches to the vine, or the bride to the bridegroom. This unity bonds us in love with the apostles, as Christ is united in love with the Father (Jn 17:23). Christ, nevertheless, lives in the Church until the end of the world (Mt 28:20). He is "yesterday, today and forever" the same (Heb 13:8), as is His Church. For Jesus Christ is present as the way, truth and Life, in the Holy Spirit, to achieve a personal, living, inner unity with the faithful. We respond to that work toward unity by our prayer, by

26  St Theophan [Feofan], "Commentary on the Epistle to the Ephesians," in *Tolkovanie...k Efeseiam*, 232.

partaking of the holy sacraments, and by seeking purity in the moral life, through the grace of the Holy Spirit at work within us. Such a life we can receive in the household of God, the one, holy Orthodox Church.

The Church is the spiritual child of divine love, divine life, divine will, divine mind and divine eternity. In the Church, God the Father, God the Son, and God the Holy Spirit exist as the source of true divine life, as life-giving power which animates and sanctifies the Church while constituting her very divine nature. The Father is in the Son, the Father and Son are in the Spirit, and the Holy Trinity dwells in the Church for the salvation of the world.

Thus, the greatest significance of the Church lies in the fact that God dwells within her upon the earth. In her essence the Church is the unity of God with men in Christ. The Church is the Body of Christ, animated and filled by the power and life of the Holy Spirit through Christ. Thereby, the Church is forever the recipient and locus of the theanthropic life of the Holy Trinity. The Church is the Kingdom of God for those who love God with their whole heart, their whole soul, and their whole mind with absolute faith. The mind of the Church is one with the mind of Christ, constantly contemplating the divine truth of God.[27]

We must always remember the spiritual essence of the Church as the unity of theanthropic life in love and truth upon the earth. However, the spiritual unity achieved with God in the Church is fully expressed in special ways: through the holy sacraments, teaching, church organization headed by the hierarchy, theology, services of sanctification, together with church art and culture. The entire sacramental life of the Church is directed toward the regeneration of man's spiritual and physical nature, in order that he might enter into the divine life of God.[28]

27  S. Verhovskoy, *Bog i chelovek* (New York, 1953), 233-236.
28  Ibid., 234.

Jesus Christ, the incarnate Son of God, "is the head of the Body, the Church. He is the beginning, the firstborn from the dead, that in all things He may have the preeminence" (Col 1:18-19); for "in Him dwelleth all the fullness of the Godhead bodily" (Col 2:9). He who lives in the love of Christ "is filled with all the fullness of God" (Eph 3:19).

Our Lord Jesus Christ was sent that we might have life. He is the Good Shepherd, who gives His life for His sheep (Jn 10:10-11). The goal of His divine, pastoral activity is that there be *one flock* and *one Shepherd* in God's Kingdom, which is now known and experienced on earth in God's Holy Orthodox Church (cf. Jn 10:16).

# 4

# The Church and the Kingdom of God

### "My Kingdom is not of this world" (Jn 18:36)

The Son of God, our Lord Jesus Christ, became incarnate "to do the will of the Father and to accomplish His work" (Jn 4:34). In order for all men to be saved and to come to the knowledge of the Truth, Jesus gave Himself as a ransom for all, to be the mediator between God and man (1 Tim 2:4-6). With the Incarnation of Jesus Christ, the Kingdom of God came into the world.

"I am the Way, the Truth and the Life; no one comes to the Father except by me," (Jn 14:6). Thus, the Lord Jesus Christ declares: In Me, in what I say and do, any person can find for himself the true way of life. In Me, a person can learn the only real and unchangeable truth. In Me is revealed for mankind the source of blessed eternal life. The incarnation of the Son of God fulfilled God's will in three divine actions: Jesus' suffering and death on the Cross; His resurrection from the dead together with His ascension and glorification at the throne of God; and His sending into the world the Holy Spirit to continue His work in His Kingdom which is the Church. In the unity of these three actions "is found the divine nature of the Church as the Kingdom of God."[1]

As the divine teacher and prophet, Jesus Christ announced the mystery of our salvation, and He showed us the direct pathway that leads from death to life. As high priest, redeemer and savior, He saved the world from sin and death and gave us the gift of son-

---

1   V. Soloviov, *Dukhovnye osnovy zhizni* ( New York, 1958), 108.

ship with God. As king, He brought His Kingdom to earth, thereby opening the doorway into eternal life in His Church.[2]

Statements of our Lord Jesus Christ concerning His Kingdom touch on two very different aspects, which complement one another. The Incarnate Son of God came to reveal His kingdom, which is not *of this world* (Jn 18:36). Yet again, on earth He founded His Church (Mt 16:18) to be the *earthly aspect* of His kingdom, embracing human creatures, both the living and the departed, who constitute the fullness of the Church (Eph 1:21-23). Both these aspects—the "other worldly" and the "worldly"—are realized by one and the same Person: Jesus Christ, the Messiah or Anointed One, who is the God-Man and Savior of the world. The origin and the nature of the kingdom of God and of the Church lie with Him, our heavenly King and Lord, together with the Holy Spirit. The Son and the Spirit work together to fulfill the will of God the Father. Thus, we affirm that the kingdom of God and the Church find their origin and purpose within the Holy Trinity.

Jesus Christ inaugurated the Church on earth with the revelation of the Good News: "The time is fulfilled and the Kingdom of God is at hand; repent and believe in the Gospel!" (Mk 1:15; Mt 4:17). The Kingdom, which for centuries had been promised to the chosen people in the Scriptures, the time foreseen by the prophet Jeremiah (31:31) became a reality in the person of Christ. The Messiah, who is King within His Kingdom, brought new life for the salvation of the world (Jn 3:6). "Blessed are the eyes which see what you see!," He declared. "For I tell you, many prophets and kings desired to see what you see and did not see it, and to hear what you hear and did not hear it" (Lk 10:23f). The Kingdom of God is the fruit of God's love: "Fear not little flock, for it is your Father's good pleasure to give you the Kingdom" (Lk 12:32).

2   On the threefold service of Jesus Christ, see Archpriest N. Malinovskii, *Ocherk pravoslavnogo dogmaticheskogo bogosloviia* (Moscow, 1911), 431-471.

The "Kingdom of God" or the "Kingdom of Heaven," which our Savior announced to the world, mainly refers to the Church of Christ. Jesus seldom used the word "Church" (*ekklesia*). In fact, only two instances appear where Jesus explains the origin and character of the Church. They can be found in the Gospel of St Matthew, 16:18 and 18:17. Most of the time, the Church is depicted or explained in the form of parables or images of the Kingdom.[3]

The theologian Rudolf Schnackenburg stated:

> The Kingdom of God in a certain way [is] already there [in the world], namely as the eschatological rule of God which became present and operative in Jesus' person and work, and perceptible and tangible in his saving powers. It was then realized in a new way as the dominion of the exalted Christ through the mission of the Spirit and found its grace-abounding presence precisely in the Church.[4]

Answering Pilate, Jesus Christ confirmed that He is the king[5] and that His kingdom is "not of this world" (Jn 18:36f). The true origin of the kingdom of God is not earthly or human; it is divine, heavenly, supernatural. Christ is king and God; therefore His kingdom is the source of new life and freedom in the Spirit (Jn 3:3, 5; 8:32, 36). Accordingly, His words, "My kingdom is not of this world," refers not to its earthly aspect marked by historical development. They refer rather to the ontological origin and foundation of the kingdom, its higher, divine origin that embraces all ages. At the same time this includes Christ's earthly kingdom, existing in the world as His divine life, power, and love. It is the kingdom that manifests itself in the Church: through the growth and development of the Body of Him who was born into the world in order to bear witness to the Truth (Jn 18:37).

---

3  Parable of the Sower (Mk 4:14-20); Parable of the Growing Seed (Mk 4:26); Parable of the Wheat and Tares (Mt 13:24-30, 36-43); Parable of the Great Supper (Lk 13:16-24); Parable of the Marriage Feast (Mt 22:2-14); The Little Flock (Lk 12:32); The Door, Shepherd, One Flock (Jn 10:1-16); The Vine and the Branches (Jn 15:1-6); The Mustard Seed (Mt 13:31f); The Net (Mt 13:47); Leaven (Mt 13:33).

4  R. Schnackenburg, *The Church in the New Testament* (New York, 1965), 188.

5  Christ was born as King (Mt 2:2; Lk 1:32f); He entered Jerusalem as King (Mt 21:9; Mk 11:10; Lk 19:28).

Jesus Christ chooses His apostles "in the world" (Jn 15:19). Yet, as He Himself is not of this world, so they too are not of this world (Jn 17:14). Therefore Jesus prays to His Father not to take them out of this world, but to "keep them from the evil one" (Jn 17:15).

What is the nature of Christ's kingdom? It is not the natural, earthly kingdom of Israel that the Hebrew people awaited for generations. His kingdom consists of those who are "poor in spirit," "meek," and "pure in heart," as well as "those who are persecuted for righteousness' sake" (Mt 5:3-10; Lk 6:20-22). It is, in essence, a spiritual kingdom.

The kingdom of God is the ultimate value: "Seek first the kingdom of God and its righteousness" (Mt 6:33; Mk 10:39-40; Lk 12:32).[6] The kingdom is compared to the "hidden treasure" and to the "pearl of great price" (Mt 13:44-46). The pathway to the kingdom leads by way of the cross of Christ (Mt 10:38; Mk 8:34; Lk 14:27). All are called to enter the kingdom (Mt 8:11f). For this reason, the Gospel of the kingdom must be proclaimed to all the world (Mt 28:16-20; Mk 13:10; Lk 24:47; Acts 1:8).

The kingdom of God is "here among you" (Lk 17:21), in the person and works of Jesus Christ and in the power of God released into the world (Mk 9:1). The power of the Devil cannot stand against the kingdom which "has come upon you" (Lk 11:20; Mt 12:28). The king Himself stands at the door and knocks (Lk 12:36; Rev 3:20).

By identifying Himself with His Church (Mt 16:18), Jesus Christ enables her to possess the spiritual powers "not of this world," for "the kingdom of God has come upon you" (Mt 12:28). It is "at hand" and it has "come with power" (Mk 1:15; 9:1). The mission of the seventy apostles is to announce that "the kingdom of God has drawn near to you," "has come upon you," and "dwells within you" (Lk 10:9; 11:20; 17:21). Those who inherit the

6   On the absolute value of the Kingdom of God, see also Lk 18:29; Mk 10:29; Mt 19:29.

kingdom must be like little children (Lk 18:16); yet an effort or "violence" is needed in order for one to enter the kingdom of God (Mt 11:12). The power of the kingdom is seen in miracles, and in the healing of every sickness and disease (Mt 9:35).

How does the Kingdom of God "live within us"? According to St Theophan the Recluse:

> The kingdom is a spiritual state in which God begins to rule in our souls through our Lord Jesus Christ. God enters into living contact with the soul, making of her His abode, giving her new life and new commandments, and restoring her to a state of goodness. To seek the "Kingdom of God" is to seek eternal blessedness with Christ in His glory at the right hand of the Father."[7]

The Church as the kingdom of God is clearly revealed in the promise of Jesus Christ to build His Church, to bestow the keys of the kingdom to the Apostle Peter, and to grant to all the apostles the power to "bind and loose" (Mt 16:18f; 18:18). Thereby, Jesus identifies His Church with the new life in His kingdom: for "he who is not born of water and the Spirit cannot enter the kingdom of God" (Jn 3:3-5). Entrance into the kingdom is identical with entrance into the Church.

The kingdom of God was prepared from all eternity (Mt 25:34). As the kingdom of God on earth, the Church has her divine roots in eternity. She was founded within the framework of human history by Jesus Christ Himself, who is the "life of the world" and "the Son of the living God" (Jn 6:51; 14:6; Mt 16:16). At its deepest level of meaning, then, the Church can be said to be the realization of the kingdom of God on earth. It is the kingdom of divine love, grace, and unity, in which faithful believers in the Son of the living God receive new life, sanctification, and salvation in God's eternal kingdom.

The kingdom of God, including God's divine rule and power, is already present and operative in the person and presence of Jesus

---

7  "Commentary on Colossians," in *Tolkovanie...k Kolossianam* (Moscow, 1892), 3:1, 158.

Christ, in His works and miracles, accomplished through the power of the Holy Spirit. It is in the Church that the power and grace of Christ's kingdom are present. Bishop Kassian has said, "The kingdom of God can be understood as the precursor of the promise of eternal fullness. It is in the Church that we find the earthly aspect of the kingdom."[8]

Jesus Christ possesses the keys to the kingdom, to death and to life: "I died, and behold I am alive for evermore, and I have the keys of Death and Hades" (Rev 1:18). He is "the Holy One, the True One, who has the key of David, who opens and no one shall shut, who shuts and no one opens" (Rev 3:7). Jesus has transferred the "key" that opens the doorway into the Kingdom of Heaven to the apostles in His Church. The Church becomes the pathway and the doorway into the Kingdom of God by receiving this "key" through the apostle Peter (Mt 16:19). Access to the Kingdom was "shut up" or closed off by the scribes and Pharisees; it is now open to all those who seek to enter and there find salvation (Mt 23:13).

According to its founder and head, the Church will not be defeated even by "the gates of hell" (Mt 16:18). This means that the saving gifts obtained through life within the Church will be offered "until the end of the world" (Mt 28:20), when the kingdom of God will come in glory.

Although she possesses God's authority, power and the fullness of Christ, the Church is not yet the kingdom of glory; for it is not the Church herself, but the kingdom of God that is the ultimate goal of the divine plan of salvation. Therefore we ceaselessly pray, "Thy kingdom come!" (Lk 11:2; Mt 5:10). The earthly Church is still a militant pilgrim in this world. She is growing as the house of the living God, as the body of Christ, striving for the measure of the fullness of Christ in glory. She awaits the "new heaven" and the "new earth"—"the holy city, new Jerusalem, coming down out of heaven from God, prepared as a bride adorned for her husband" (Rev 21:2).

8   Bishop Kassian Bezobrazov, *Khristos i pervoe khristianskoe pokoleni* (Paris, 1950), 40.

Meanwhile, Scripture reminds us that the members of the Church can become lukewarm, "neither hot nor cold" (Rev 3:15-16), and that they can stand under the judgment of God (Rom 2:2-5; 14:10; 1 Cor 4:5; 2 Cor 5:10). The parable of the wheat and the tares clearly explains that the good and righteous will exist in the Church together with those who are evil. This condition will endure until the end of the world, when all will be judged according to their life and works (Mt 13:24-30, 36-43; cf. Mt 25:31-46). The kingdom of God is already here among us, yet it is still to come. It is both a present reality and a future hope.

The relationship of the Church to the kingdom of God is beautifully expressed by the author of the *Didache* or *Teaching of the Twelve Apostles* (early second century):

Remember, O Lord, Thy Church. Preserve her from all evil and make her perfect in Thy love. Gather the sanctified Church from the four corners of the earth into Thy kingdom, which Thou hast prepared for her![9]

Evidence of this striving towards the kingdom of God is most apparent in the sacrament of the Eucharist: "I say to you," Jesus declares to His disciples at the Last Supper, "I will drink no more of the fruit of the vine until that day when I drink it new in the kingdom of God" (Mk 14:25; Lk 22:16). In the Eucharist, the entire assembly of the Church—including the prophets, apostles, martyrs and saints—"seems to ascend to heaven, elevated and lifted up by Christ to His table in His Kingdom."[10]

The divine power, life, unity, and love of the kingdom of God is present in the world; it is even "within" us (Lk 17:21). Having founded His Church, Jesus Christ has now transferred the authority of the Kingdom of God to His disciples and apostles, in order to continue through them His work of salvation within the world: "I assign to you, as my Father assigned to me, a Kingdom..." (Lk 22:29).

9 "Didache, or Teaching of the Twelve Apostles," in *The Ante-Nicene Fathers: Translations of The Writings of the Fathers down to AD 325*, vol. 7 (Grand Rapids, 1963), 380.
10 Archpriest Alexander Schmemann, *The Eucharist—Sacrament of the Kingdom* (Crestwood, 1988), 21.

It seems appropriate to conclude this chapter on the relation of the Church to the Kingdom of God with a definition taken from the writings of A.S. Pavlov:

> For believers in Jesus Christ, the Church is the divine institution directly founded by Christ Himself. In the Church and through the Church the reality of the Kingdom of God is revealed to men on earth. In the Church the knowledge of God is preserved, while gifts of grace and power are given to the faithful for their spiritual growth, in order to bring their own will into harmony with the will of God, for the purpose of unity with God in life eternal.[11]

11  A.S. Pavlov, *Kurs tserkovnogo prava* (Moscow, 1902), 5.

# 5

# The Church of Jesus Christ

**"I will build my church; and the gates of hell shall
not prevail against it" (Mt 16:18)**

The Church-*Ecclesia* is the gathering of those who are the "chosen generation." It is the society of those who have heard and accepted the call of our Lord Jesus Christ for salvation, those who confess Him to be the Son of the living God (Mt 16:16). He came as the incarnate Lord, to gather together as one those in heaven and on earth (Eph 1:10): "For the Son of Man is come to save that which was lost" (Mt 18:11). Jesus Christ and His Kingdom is the source of life for the Church Herself. The Church is the *realization* and the *continuation* of the saving work of Christ in the world.

Thus, the earthly, visible Church of Christ is the society of people who truly believe in Jesus Christ, and who constitute His mystical, spiritual Body. Through faith, the sacraments and its hierarchy, under the power of the Holy Spirit and the invisible authority of Christ Himself, the Church continues until the end of the world. It carries forth the work of sanctification and salvation of the faithful begun by our savior and redeemer during His earthly life, with the purpose and goal of guiding all people along the pathway towards eternal life in the Kingdom of God.

The true meaning of the Church can only be found in the teaching, actions, and decisions of Jesus Christ. When He came into the region of Caesarea Philippi, Jesus asked His disciples, "Who do the people say that I am?" They answered that the crowds think Him to be either John the Baptist, Elijah, Jeremiah, or one of the other prophets, returned to life. Evidently Jesus was not satisfied with their answer, for He then rephrased the question: "And who do you say that I am?" The apostle Peter, replying in the name of all the apostles, confessed: "You are the Christ, the Son of the living God" (Mt 16:13-16).

In response to this confession, Jesus pronounced Peter "blessed," since this truth was revealed to him, not by flesh and blood, but by "my Father who is in heaven." Then He added: "And you are Peter [*petros*], and on this rock [*petra*] I will build my Church, and the gates of Hell shall not prevail against it" (Mt 16:17f).

Bishop Sylvester interprets the words of Jesus Christ concerning the Apostle Peter's confession, in this way: "Your confession is hard and firm as a rock. Therefore I call you Peter; and on this rock-solid confession I will build my Church." And he continues: "If beneath the [image of the] rock on which the Church was to be built there stands the person of the Apostle Peter, then Peter may be called 'the rock of the Church,' inasmuch as his confession of faith made him to be a rock."[1]

On the same subject St Augustine declares that the Church is founded upon a rock [*petra*], from which Peter received his name: "For *petra* (rock) is not derived from Peter, but Peter from *petra*, just as Christ is not called such from 'Christian,' but 'Christian' is derived from Christ. On this account the Lord said, 'On this rock I will build my Church,' because Peter had confessed, 'Thou art the Christ, the Son of the living God.' On this rock of Peter's confession He said He would build His Church. For the Rock [*petra*] was Christ, and Peter himself was also built on this foundation."[2]

1  Bishop Sylvester [Unknown], *Uchenie o Tserkvi v pervie tri veka Khristianstva* (Kiev, 1872), 12.
2  St Augustine, "Commentary on the Gospel of John," 21:5. It is interesting to note that out of eighty-five Church Fathers, forty-four understand the "rock" to be the Apostle Peter's confession. Seventeen understand Peter himself to be the rock, and sixteen understand the rock to be Christ, whereas eight hold that the rock refers to the Apostles. See L. Epifanovich, *Zapiski po oblechitelnomu bogosloviu* (Novocherkask, 1904), 49.

Thus it is faith in Jesus Christ, the Son of the living God—a firm, true and living faith revealed not by flesh and blood, or by earthly desires and impulses, but by God the Father—that, according to Christ Himself, becomes the foundation of His Church on earth. By bestowing on Peter the keys to the Kingdom of Heaven, Christ presented the Church to the world as the divinely-founded society of salvation—His Kingdom (cf. Mk 1:15; 9:1; Mt 3:2; 4:17; 12:21; Lk 9:2; 10:9; 11:20; 17:21; 18:16; 22:29f).

Not only was the Church founded by the will of Christ, by His power and love, but He is the foundation, the cornerstone and the head of the Church, which He purchased with His own blood (Acts 20:28). And His Church, as the Kingdom of the Spirit and of freedom, is open to all mankind, without national, political, ethnic or social limitations within time and space, for Jesus Christ abides with His Church until the end of the world (Mt 16:18; 28:20; Lk 17:21).

Speaking of the relationship of Jesus Christ to His Church, St Theophan the Recluse declares:

> Christ fulfills the Church. His light of knowledge is innate to the Church. His holiness is granted to those who love holiness. He is compassionate and blesses those who are merciful. To Him belongs every visible, spiritual gift within the Church, for through those gifts He saves the faithful. In the Church, Christ is everything: He is all in all.[3]

Truly Jesus Christ, dwelling within the Church, is the source of the Church's divine life (Jn 15:1-6), which flows into the Church as from the head into the body (Eph 4:15f).

The work of the Son of God for the salvation of the world embraces the whole life of the Church on earth. This work cannot be fully and completely described, for "even the world itself could not contain all the books that should be written" (Jn 21:25). Nevertheless, in the Holy Scriptures we know our Lord Jesus Christ to be the Prophet and Messiah, who called Himself the only Teacher

3 "Commentary on Ephesians," in *Tolkovaniia...k Efesiam* (Moscow, 1893), 1:22f, 125.

and Master (Mt 23:8-10). The reason for His incarnation was so that He might teach the truth (Jn 18:37). As Prophet, Jesus was "mighty in deed and word before God and all the people" (Lk 24:19), preaching the gospel of the Kingdom and healing every sickness and disease (Mt 9:35).

The incarnate Son of God was sent to be "a merciful and faithful high priest in things pertaining to God, to make reconciliation for the sins of the people" (Heb 2:17). Jesus Christ came to save us and to give His life as a ransom for many (Mt 20:28; Mk 10:45). We are saved by the Cross of Christ, which is the power of God (1 Cor 1:17f). We are saved by the sacrifice of the Body and Blood of Jesus Christ in the Eucharist, the sacrament which grants us unity with Christ Himself: "This cup is the New Testament [Covenant] in My Blood, which is shed for you" (Lk 22:20; Mt 26:28). The bread that I give is "My flesh, which I give for the life of the world; He that eats My flesh and drinks My blood will live in Me and I in him" (Jn 6:56, 57).

As the result of His death on the Cross, Jesus Christ was glorified through His resurrection, His ascension into heaven, and His sitting at the right hand of God the Father. He was exalted in His human nature, receiving authority and power in heaven and on earth as the intercessor before God (cf. 1 Jn 2:1f). Jesus opened to redeemed humanity, the means of salvation in and through the Church, by which we receive the fruits of His redeeming work.

Jesus Christ "came down from heaven" (Jn 3:13) and entered the world to do the will of God (Heb 10:7). He gave His apostles an example, that they should do as He did to them (Jn 13:15), He who is "humble and lowly in heart" (Mt 11:29). He Himself embodied the moral ideal of perfection, whose origin is in God the Father (Mt 5:48) as it is in Himself, whose words shall never pass away (Mt 24:35). He gave a new commandment, "that you love one another as I have loved you" (Jn 13:34; 15:12, 13, 17), even to the point of loving your enemies (Mt 5:44).

Possessing the divine qualities of the Holy Trinity, the Church of Christ can only be One. The existence of two or more Churches contradicts the very nature of the Church as the unity of divine-human life. Therefore Jesus Christ speaks of His Church, which gathers all newly born people into organic unity with Himself, as the vine and the branches (Jn 15:4-6). The people of God constitute one flock with one Shepherd (Jn 10:1-10); "they are all brethren [in unity]" with Him and the Father (Mt 23:8; Jn 17:21).

Being One, the Church is by nature Catholic, embracing the whole world and existing without limitations. Jesus Christ came to save the *whole* world (Jn 3:16). He is the light of the World (Jn 1:9) and the light of life (Jn 8:12). All nations will be able to enter into His kingdom (Lk 13:29), and the Gospel of the kingdom will be witnessed and preached to all nations and to all the world (Mt 24:14).

The Church of Christ can be called the society, the institution, the community, the "little flock" of people in unity with God. The membership of the Church must strive toward moral perfection and salvation by conquering their sinful nature and by becoming newly born into a new life by water and the Spirit (Jn 3:5). It is this Spirit who will guide the Church into "all the truth" (Jn 16:13).

The incarnation of the Son of God and the descent of the Holy Spirit into the world reveal the will and love of God the Father for us. They manifest the humility and glory of Jesus Christ and make the introduction of the Church into the divine life by the Spirit possible. In its essence the Church is the unity of theanthropic life, and as such she belongs to the heavenly realm as "the Kingdom not of this world" (Jn 18:36). Yet even within human history the Church exists as the Kingdom of the beloved Son of God (Col 1:13-20).

Jesus Christ chose the Twelve to be with Him as apostles, messengers sent to proclaim His Good News (Lk 6:13). They were called to be living witnesses of the greatest revelation of God to the world: the incarnation of God's Son, who established the kingdom of God on earth for the salvation of the world. Jesus Himself chose those whom He desired (Jn 15:16), that He might send them to preach and to be "fishers of men" (Mt 4:19).

To the apostles Jesus Christ explained the mysteries of the kingdom of God (Mk 4:11), of faith (Mt 17:20), and of the exercise of authority (Mt 20:25-28). He explained all things to them in private (Mk 4:34), making known to them what He had heard from the Father (Jn 15:15). His disciples beheld the Lord's power over death (Mk 5:35-41), over nature (Mk 4:38), and over the Sabbath (Mt 12:8). Jesus sent them into the world to proclaim the coming of the kingdom of God (Mt 10:7; Lk 9:6), with the promise that the Spirit would help them (Mk 13:11) and remind them of His teaching (Jn 14:26). He reminded them that they would be hated in the world; yet promised those who endure to the end for Christ's sake "will be saved" (Mk 13:13; Mt 24:13).

The establishment of a hierarchical principle within the Church is rooted in the action of God the Father, who "transferred us into the kingdom of His beloved Son" (Col 1:13). Jesus Christ assigned to His apostles the kingdom, as His Father assigned it to Him (Lk 22:29). He also commissioned them: "As my Father has sent Me, even so do I send you." And having said this, He breathed upon them and said, "Receive the Holy Spirit" (Jn 20:21f). By the power of the Holy Spirit the apostles were given authority to remit sins or to retain them (Jn 20:23). This Spirit is the "other Comforter" who will abide with them forever (Jn 14:16) and guide them into all the Truth (Jn 16:13). Likewise Jesus Himself will abide with them (Jn 14:18), authorizing and empowering them to teach, to baptize, and to accomplish all that He commanded. Thus He transfers to His apostles His own authority in heaven and on earth (Mt 28:16-20) and lays the foundation for its transmission in the Church through "apostolic succession." Thereby the Church was given authority to exercise judgment (Mt 18:16f).

In the witness of the Holy Scriptures we find the Church of Christ to be "the divinely founded institution of the newly born, regenerated, and redeemed people who believe in Jesus Christ as the Son of the living God. They are united to Him by divine life and love as well as by the holy sacraments, and strive for perfection under the permanent guidance of the Holy Spirit."[4] According to Protopresbyter Alexander Schmemann, the Church's humanity is not independent of her spiritual essence or divine root; rather, it embodies it, expresses it, and is totally and absolutely subordinated to it.[5]

In summary, we can affirm the following: The Church of Christ as the realization (i.e., the aspect, embodiment, and actualization) of the kingdom of Christ on earth unites in Herself the freedom, holiness, love, truth, and life of Jesus Christ and all the qualities of the kingdom of God, including power, justice, beauty, and joy in the Holy Spirit. The Church, as the Kingdom of Christ, embraces the whole cosmos and unites all heavenly and earthly powers under the supreme rule of God. The Church, as the instrument of Christ's Kingdom in the world, provides the opportunity to partake of the redeeming fruits of the saving work of Christ to all people, by offering them new life, sanctification, sacramental grace, and moral perfection in the Holy Spirit.

Finally, the saving work of Jesus Christ reaches its fulfillment in His ascension and in the sending of the Holy Spirit upon the apostles. The task given to the Son by the Father is accomplished: "I have glorified Thee on earth; I have finished the work Thou gavest me to do... Glorify me, O Father, with the glory which I

---

4   V. Troitskii, *Ocherki iz istorii dogmata o Tserkvi* (Moscow, 1913), 10f.
5   A. Schmemann, "The Church is Hierarchical," *Report to All-American Council* (1963), 36, 37.

had with you before the world was" (Jn 17:4f). This man Jesus, the Epistle to the Hebrews declares, offered "a single sacrifice for sins, [then] sat down at the right hand of God" (10:12). The road from heaven to earth and from earth to heaven will be open forever, thanks to the descent of the Holy Spirit, who is both in heaven and in the earthly Church of Christ (Acts 1:4-8; Lk 24:49). The promise of the Holy Spirit and the commission to the apostles to be witnesses of Jesus Christ from Jerusalem to the ends of the earth is now being fulfilled. They undertake their mission, accompanied by Jesus' promise: "He who receives you, receives Me; and he who receives Me, receives Him who sent Me" (Mt 10:40; Jn 13:20).

# 6

# The Church of the Apostles

**"And they were all filled with the Holy Spirit..."**
**(Acts 2:4)**

The descent of the Holy Spirit upon the apostles at Pentecost was the day when new life, the power of God, entered into the world. At this moment the promise of Jesus Christ to build His Church on earth, as the "Kingdom of God not of this world," became a reality. On Pentecost, the Old Testament promise uttered by the prophet Joel concerning the outpouring of the Holy Spirit was fulfilled by our Lord Jesus Christ (Acts 2:16-17). The Day of the Lord has come, and "whosoever shall call on the name of the Lord shall be saved" (2:20-21). On Pentecost, the nucleus of the Church—a "little flock" of 120 believers in Jesus Christ—became the seed from which grew new life for the salvation of the whole world, through the descent of the Holy Spirit.

In accordance with the commandments of Christ, the apostles were in Jerusalem, waiting "with one accord" for the descent of the Holy Spirit from heaven (Acts 1:4). As promised to the apostles by God the Father, the Holy Spirit was sent upon them as a "rushing, mighty wind" from heaven, to appear upon them as "tongues of fire." They were all "filled with the Holy Spirit," and began, under the inspirational power of the Spirit, to "speak in other tongues" (Acts 2:1-4).

This was indeed the "baptism of the faithful," when the seal of Christ's victory and glory, "the power from on high," entered into the world (Lk 24:49; Acts 1:4-5). As the source of divine life, the kingdom of God now found its continuation in the world with the descent of the Holy Spirit. The Spirit revealed Himself as the "other Comforter," dwelling in the apostles to bear witness to the Son of God, to reveal His glory, and to seal His victory (Jn 15:26; 16:7, 14). In the person of the Holy Spirit, the glorified Christ returned to His flock, to abide with them forever. "I will not abandon you, I shall come to you!" (Jn 14:18; Mt 28:20).

At Pentecost, the apostle Peter spoke these words concerning the Lord Jesus Christ: "Being exalted at the right hand of God, and having received from the Father the promise of the Holy Spirit, He has poured out this which you see and hear" (Acts 2:33). The same Holy Spirit through whom "the Word became flesh," now at Pentecost animates the gathering of the apostles. He makes of them the nucleus of the Church and instruments of God within the world, to set forth God's work for the salvation of the world. He makes of them the Body of Christ, for through the operation of the Holy Spirit in baptism, the faithful are incorporated into the Body of Christ (1 Cor 12:23).

From the very beginning the apostolic Church reflects the ideal of the universal Church of Christ, for the apostles followed not their own will, but the instructions and will of Jesus Christ, "to observe all that I have commanded you," that is, "things pertaining to the Kingdom of God" (Mt 28:20; Acts 1:3). Therefore we can see in the actions of the apostles a living witness to the will of Christ for His Church. The Church of Christ, as a divinely founded society, continues to reveal her Founder in the world, even though Christ has ascended into heaven. This is because, as the Scripture declares, "Jesus Christ is the same yesterday, today and forever" (Heb 13:8).

After Pentecost the "little flock" quickly grew into the large, strong Body of Christ, with three then five thousand new members (Acts 2:41; 4:4). This Body constituted one perfect, spiritual organism, united by the new faith and the new life in the Holy Spirit. This was truly the Church of Christ, since it is He who acted invisibly within her and animated her life, just as He had promised (Mt 16:18).

The will of Jesus Christ in the early Church is manifested in His sending of the Holy Spirit upon the apostles, to make of them His witnesses from Jerusalem to the ends of the world (Acts 1:8). The election of Matthias to the apostleship, to serve as successor to the fallen Judas, was the doing of the Lord, "who knows the hearts of all men" (Acts 1:23-24).

That it was the Lord Jesus Christ Himself who united newly baptized Christians in "one heart and one soul" is evident from the beautiful description given of the first Jerusalem Church in Acts 2:42-47.

> They continued steadfastly in the apostolic doctrine and fellowship, in the breaking of bread, and in prayer....And many wonders and signs were done through the apostles. And all who believed were together and had all things in common; and they sold their possessions and goods and distributed them to all, as any had need. And day by day, attending the temple together and breaking bread in their homes, they partook of food with glad and generous hearts, praising God and having favor with all the people. And the Lord added to the Church day by day those who were being saved.

This provides us with an excellent picture of the apostolic Church, the divinely founded society of believers in Jesus Christ, living and growing together in harmony, and marked with the invisible seal and presence of Christ and the Holy Spirit.

We can say that Jesus Christ Himself, in response to faith in Him as Lord and Christ (Acts 2:36) and by the grace of the Holy Spirit, unites to Himself faithful believers. Christ works within the inner life of believers, upon their hearts and souls; and He does so through the power of the Holy Spirit (Acts 2:33-39).

The Church of God belongs to Jesus Christ and the Holy Spirit, for she was "purchased" by Christ, "with His own blood." Within the Church of Christ, the Holy Spirit also calls and consecrates bishops for the purpose of "feeding" the Church (Acts 20:28).

Although the apostle Paul was chosen directly by Jesus Christ (whom the apostle had persecuted!), he was nevertheless sent, after being baptized by Ananias, to receive confirmation and acceptance from the authorities of the Church (Acts 9:15-17).

At Pentecost, the Church of Christ became a reality, thus revealing the fact that Christianity has never existed apart from the Church. At the time of the Spirit's descent upon the community of faith, the New Testament scriptures had not yet been written, but the Church existed, empowered by God's living Word and His Holy Spirit.

The rule and authority of Jesus Christ within the Church was entrusted not to the world in general, but by the Holy Spirit it was communicated to the apostles and to their successors, as new members of the Church were delivered into the eternal Kingdom of Christ (Col 1:13).

Jesus Christ gave His apostles the authority to build His Church on earth. They accepted this task by witnessing to His resurrection, by teaching the Word of God (Acts 1:8; 2:14-41; 4:2), by preaching Jesus Christ everywhere (5:42; 6:2-4), and by building the Church through their missionary activity (9:32; 11:19-21; 14:20-21; 19:21).

From the very beginning the first Church, the Church of Jerusalem, was orderly and hierarchical. The apostles, who received the authority from Jesus to bind and loose (to retain or remit sins), stand at the center of the Church's life. They are the source of her unity and govern her whole life and mission. They baptize new Christians, serve the Eucharist, lay on hands in "ordination" on bishops, presbyters and deacons, persevere in mission work, and care for the pastoral needs of new members. Thus believers, through faith, baptism and the seal of the Holy Spirit, became constituent members of the Church of Christ.

Since its inception on the day of Pentecost the Church of the apostles lived—as she continues to live—by the divine life imparted to her by her Founder. It is this life that orders and structures the Church. Therefore the Church of Christ in our present day is one with the Church of the apostles, in her essence, her task, her goal, and her hierarchical ordering.

The apostles practiced the laying on of hands to ordain or consecrate deacons (Acts 6:1-6) and presbyters (Acts 14:23). The Jerusalem Council (Acts 15) held by the apostles, became the prototype for all Church councils by basing itself on a formula that was ideal for the solving of problems: "For it seemed good to the Holy Spirit and to us" (Acts 15:28, etc.).

After this brief look at the Acts of the Apostles, we can conclude that the Church which Jesus Christ promised to build, found its beginning at the moment of the feast of Pentecost. She is Christ's Church, the society of those who believe in Him as Lord and God. The Church is a spiritual organism. Indeed, she can be called the Kingdom of the Holy Spirit, in that she is marked by truth, grace and moral perfection. Her goal, finally, is to bring the faithful into blessed union with God through her sacramental life.

In several epistles of the holy apostles, we also discover a witness to the divine origin and the divine nature of the Church of Christ.

In the writings of the apostles, and especially in the epistles of St Paul, we find many images depicting the divine origin and the divine nature of the Church, images that were taken from family life, from building or from agriculture. The apostle Paul reveals the essence of the Church as the one undivided, divine-human Body of Christ. This Body comprises not only all those believers who live on earth and those who are departed. It also embraces the saints, the angelic hosts, and all past and future generations (Eph 1:21-23; 4:4-7, 11-12; 5:23, 32; Heb 12:22-24). Furthermore, in the apostolic writings we see that Jesus is not only the founder of the Church; He is also the head of his body—the Church—which possesses the whole fullness of Christ.

The epistles speak of the "Church of God" (1 Cor 1:2; 10:32; 15:9) as the "holy temple in the Lord" (Eph 2:21), the "dwelling place of God in the Holy Spirit" (Eph 2:22). The Church is "the house of God" (1 Pet 4:17), and the members of that house constitute "the temple of the living God, [and] as God said, I will live in them and move among them, and I will be their God, and they shall be my people" (2 Cor 6:16). "Do you not know," the apostle asks rhetorically, "that your body is the temple of the Holy Spirit, who is in you?" (1 Cor 6:19). Christians become temples of God, because God enters into them with His divine power. He abides in them, just as He abides in His house: "I have sanctified the house which you have built to put my name there forever. And my eyes and my heart shall be there always" (1 Kgs 9:3).

Thus the essence of the house or temple of God lies in the special presence of God, with His divine power and life. When He blesses the temple of Solomon, God explains this to us: "I will abide in the midst of the children of Israel" (1 Kgs 6:13). The Church, consisting of the "elect," an "incorruptible inheritance," "the people of God" and His chosen "flock" (1 Pet 1:2-4; 2:10; 5:3-4), is the new house of Israel, founded upon a new covenant (Heb 8:8). Thus the Church, founded by Jesus Christ (Mt 16:18) is the temple or house of God, in which our redeemer and savior lives and through which He acts in the world for our salvation through the Holy Spirit.

The first letter to Timothy (3:15) describes how one ought to behave "in the house of God, which is the church of the living God, the pillar and foundation of truth." St Theophan the Recluse comments on this passage:

> The Church possesses the living God, being animated by Him through living unity. She truly experiences His presence, and therefore the Church is His House. God created for Himself a House out of human souls, by calling, purifying and sanctifying them. Fulfilling all things in Himself, He unites all in a oneness of life: those yet living and those who have departed are embraced in a single living unity." He contin-

ues, "The Church is the pillar and foundation of Truth, for it is the Church of the living God, who is the Truth itself. Therefore everything in the Church is of Truth: true confession of faith, true sacraments, true gifts of grace, true divine life imparted to those who live by God, true divine miracles and power: all becomes Truth within the Church.[1]

According to the apostle Paul, the Church is the building of God (1 Cor 3:9), the "dwelling place of God in the Spirit" (Eph 2:22), built on the stone which the builders rejected, but which has become the cornerstone (Mt 21:42; Acts 4:11; 1 Pet 2:17). Our Lord Jesus Christ is the one and only true foundation of the Church: "For no other foundation can any one lay than that which is laid, which is Jesus Christ" (1 Cor 3:11). Jesus Christ is Himself the chief cornerstone (Eph 2:20). Every member enters the Church to become a "living stone" (1 Pet 2:5) that contributes to the building up of the temple of God, whose founder and foundation is Jesus Christ, the first cause and divine origin of the Church.

Jesus Christ is the cornerstone of the Church in a very particular way, for as her Redeemer He gave himself on the cross to purchase the Church "with His own blood" (Acts 20:28), to reconcile man with God by His death, that man might thereby receive salvation and atonement (Rom 5:10, 11).

As the cornerstone and foundation of the one holy catholic Church, fully actualized in every local church community, Jesus Christ fills the Church with His divine power and strength, that she might grow into a holy temple in the Lord (Eph 2:21).

According to the apostles, members of the Church of Christ are the "people of God," the offspring of the woman of the Apocalypse "who keep the commandments of God" (Rev 12:17). They are a "chosen generation, a royal priesthood, a holy nation, God's own people" who proclaim the promise of Him who called them "out of darkness into His marvelous light" (1 Pet 2:9-10). They

---

1    St Theophan [Feofan], "Commentary on the Pastoral Epistles," in *Tolkovaniia na poslaniia sv. apostola Pavla* (Moscow, 1893), 309.

constitute "the house of God" (1 Pet 4:17), whose members, according to St Paul, are "no longer strangers and foreigners, but fellow citizens with the saints and members of the household of God," build together for a "dwelling place of God in the Spirit" (Eph 2:19-22).

Thus the Church, the gathering together of the people of God into a single reality, is by its character, it goal, and its relations to God, absolutely different from any human, earthly society. For being "fellow citizens with the saints and members of the household of God," Christians who live as members of the earthly Church belong already to the heavenly realm as members of the "kingdom of [God's] beloved Son" (Col 1:13) and constitute a "holy temple in the Lord" (Eph 2:21).

On earth the Church possesses no permanent city in which to dwell, but she seeks "one to come" (Heb 13:14). Through Jesus Christ, the second Adam and bearer of new, divine life (1 Cor 15:45), both the living and the departed members of the Church are already citizens of the Heavenly Jerusalem. It is there that the divine-human nature of the Church is most perfectly revealed: "Come to Mount Zion and to the city of the living God, the heavenly Jerusalem, to an innumerable company of angels, to the general assembly and church of the firstborn who are registered in heaven, to God the judge of all, to the spirits of just men made perfect, to Jesus who is the mediator of the New Covenant" (Heb 12:22-24). Truly this is a magnificent vision of the divine-human nature of the one catholic Church: the Church is the city of God, the heavenly Jerusalem, headed by God who is judge of all. The Church consists of all the firstborn, united in heaven with the souls of the righteous made perfect. It is into such a city that believers enter who seek the eternal building of God in heaven (2 Cor 5:1; Col 3:2-3). Thus the Christian is at once a citizen of the one earthly Church and the one heavenly Church of Christ, a member of the Lord's undivided body (Eph 4:4-6).

St Augustine confirms this apostolic witness when he speaks of the Church which is the body of Christ: "not simply the Church that is in this particular place, but both the Church that is here and the Church which extends over the whole earth; not simply the Church that is living today, but the whole race of saints, from Abel down to all those who will ever be born and will believe in Christ until the end of the world, for all belong to one City. This City is the Body of Christ: the Whole Christ, Christ united with the Church."[2]

According to the apostle Paul, the Church is the body, of which Jesus Christ is the head. It is a single living organism, united by divine-human life (Eph 1:22; 4:4, 12, 15-16, 25; 5:23, 30; Col 1:18, 24; 2:19; 3:15; Rom 12:4-5; 1 Cor 6:15; 10:17; 12:13-27). The body possesses all the divine powers of sanctification which belong to the head. St Theophan the Recluse explains: "As the members of our bodies together with the head constitute one living organism which is ruled by the head, so also believers through their baptism are integrated into Christ—they "put on Christ"—by the power of the Holy Spirit. Thus they are created together with Him into one divine-human organism, the Church; and thus they are truly 'members of Christ'" (1 Cor 6:15).[3]

The apostle Paul thus presents for our edification a most majestic vision of the consequences of God's plan for our salvation in Jesus Christ:

...which he accomplished in Christ when He raised Him from the dead and made Him sit at His right hand in the heavenly places, far above all rule and authority and power and dominion, and above every name that is named, not only in this age but also in that which is to come; and He has put all things under His feet and has made Him the Head over

2  St Augustine, "Psalm 90, Sermon Two," in Mersch, *The Whole Christ* (Milwaukee, 1938), 415.
3  St Theophan, "Commentary on the Epistle to the Ephesians," in *Tolkovanie...k Efesiam* (Moscow, 1893), 123.

all things for the Church, which is His Body, the fullness of Him who fills all in all (Eph 1:20-23).

Reacting to this passage, St John Chrysostom offers these amazing words:

> Whereto God raised the Church? As though He were lifting it up by some engine, He has raised it up to a vast height, and set it there on the throne: for where the Head is, there is the Body also. There is no interval to separate between the Head and the Body. The fullness of Christ is the Church: and rightly, for the complement of the Head is the Body, and the complement of the Body is the Head.[4]

The Church as all-embracing fullness, is where the head is, sharing in Christ's glory and authority in heaven and on earth. On earth the Church is the vehicle or the institution, where Christ the Redeemer and Savior incorporates into His believers the most intimate unity of love and life.

The Church, according to St Augustine, is Christ: "inasmuch He is present in all places, and bears all humanity in Himself. The whole Christ is the head and the body. He is one principle, one source, one head, from which Christians derive the fullness of the divine life."[5]

Elsewhere St Paul explains the reason for such preeminence: "He is the head of the body, the Church; He is the beginning, the firstborn from the dead, that in everything He might be preeminent." For it pleased the Father "to reconcile all things to Himself through Him, whether things on earth or things in heaven, making peace by the blood of His cross" (Col 1:18-20).

The unity of the head and the body is clearly shown in the writings of Origen. He states, "The Church is the body of Christ. But must we consider it as the trunk, distinct from the head and governed by it? Or is it not the entire Church of Christ, rather the body of Christ animated by His divinity and filled with His

---

4   St. John Chrysostom, "Commentary on Ephesians," in *Tvoreniia* (St Petersburg, 1896), Homily 3.
5   St Augustine, in Mersch, *The Whole Christ*, 393, 396, 432.

Spirit, after the analogy of the human body, of which the head is itself a part?"[6]

The unity of Christ with the Church is "a great mystery" (Eph 5:32) in which the faithful spiritually and organically are incorporated into Christ, being animated, sanctified, and eventually saved by His divine power.

The Church as the body of Christ is "the fullness of Him who fills all in all" (Eph 1:23). This "fullness" (in Greek, *plerôma*) can be understood in two ways: as the fullness that fulfills, or as the fullness which is fulfilled. In both ways the mystery is truly wonderful.

Jesus Christ, the head of the Church, is the fullness of all creation on earth and in heaven (Eph 1:3; Col 1:17; 1 Cor 8:6). He himself is the absolute fullness of "all in all" as the head of the Church, His body. This body lives and breathes by Him, it is ruled by Him, and it exists for the purpose of completing the work of Christ on earth. Thus the Church is constantly *becoming* the fullness of "all in all" through its Head. Christ fills the Body with all His divine qualities and powers, animating her permanently by His presence and by His living Spirit.

On the other hand, the body completes the head, for even the perfect head remains incomplete without the body. Christ, the redeemer and savior, receives fulfillment in His body, the Church. Thus it can be said that the unity of the head and the body is the *sine qua non*, the necessary condition for the fulfillment of God's plan of salvation.

This understanding of the body of Christ as constituting Christ's fullness enables us to see that the Church is a reality that extends beyond any concrete visible, human institution or society. For the body of Christ embraces all earthly and heavenly powers, since it is also the heavenly Jerusalem (Heb 12:22-23).

6   "Contra Celsum," in *The Ante-Nicene Fathers: Translations of The Writings of the Fathers down to AD325*, (Grand Rapids, MI, 1963), vol. 2, 6:48.

Christ is the head of the Church, which is His body. The body lives by the divine life of the head. It grows and develops through its head, which is the divine principle of its life (Eph 4:16), "from whom all the body, nourished and knit together by joints and ligaments, grows with the increase that is from God" (Col 2:19). The final goal of the Church is to pursue this growth "until we all come to the unity of the faith and of the knowledge of the Son of God, to a perfect manhood, to the measure of the stature of the fullness of Christ" (Eph 4:13).

The Church as the living body of Christ consists of a multitude of members, spiritually and organically united to each other and to their head. Every member essentially is needed for every other, and all together they form the Church: "For as we have many members in one body, but all the members do not have the same function, so we, being many, are one body in Christ and individually members of one another," having different gifts according to the grace given to us, in proportion to our faith (Rom 12:4-6).

As St Paul's first letter to the Corinthians makes clear (12:12-27), the diversity of members of the body is not simply an image of beauty; it is an essential condition of the life of the Church. We are all members of one another, St Paul says. The members are not strangers to one another but are members of one body, working together in one accord. Each member is essential to maintain the health of all. "For just as the body is one and has many members, and all the members of the body, though many, are one body, so it is with Christ" (1 Cor 12:12).

The unity of the Church thus lies in its multiplicity. It is a "unity in diversity." Not every member of the body is equal in service, for "to each of us grace was given, according to the measure of Christ's gift" (Eph 4:7). But all members are needed to serve the whole body, each member supporting every other. Each is indispensable. The unity of all is neither juridical nor mechanical. It is a spiritual, organic unity, created through baptism and nurtured through faith, new life and love in the one body, which is animated by the one Spirit, with one hope: "one Lord, one faith, one baptism, one God and Father of all, who is above all, and through all, and in all" (Eph 4:4-6).

Jesus Christ, who ascended into heaven, bestows upon the Church all that is necessary for her existence and growth. "His gifts were that some should be apostles, some prophets, some evangelists, some pastors and teachers, to equip the saints for the work of ministry, for building up the body of Christ, with the goal of achieving the "measure of the stature of the fullness of Christ" (Eph 4:10-13).

Jesus Christ is the head of the Church and the savior of the body. The Church is subject to Christ, who loves her and gave Himself for her. Through His saving action the one unique Church, the body of Christ, is holy, glorious, without blemish, "not having spot or wrinkle, or any such thing." The members of his body may be likened to his very flesh. The Lord nourishes and cherishes the Church as his own flesh, united to Him in the most intimate possible relationship, for "no man ever hated his own flesh." The unity of Christ with his members, then, is the "great mystery": the Whole Christ is both head and body, each one completing and fulfilling the other (Eph 5:23-30).

Love is the essential quality that permeates the body of Christ, for it was the love and sacrifice of Christ that gave birth to the Church. By His love the Church is "nourished" and "cherished" (Eph 5:2, 25, 29). And through knowledge of the love of Christ, the "fullness of God" is achieved (Eph 3:19).

The life-giving soul of the body of Christ is the Holy Spirit. The Holy Spirit dwells in the Church and in each faithful Christian, who is His temple (1 Cor 3:16; 6:19). For it was through the descent of the Holy Spirit that the "little flock" of Christ became the Church of Christ on the day of Pentecost. This indwelling presence of the

Spirit makes the true life of the Church spiritual in its nature and divine in its origin. The Holy Spirit is the principle of the life and activity of the Church (1 Cor 12:3-11). The Church is one body in Christ and one in the Spirit (Eph 4:4). By the Spirit of the Lord, Christians can grow "from glory to glory" into the image of the Lord (2 Cor 3:18), for "he who is joined to the Lord is one Spirit" with Him (1 Cor 6:17). By the one Spirit we are all baptized into the one body, receiving new life in Christ (1 Cor. 12:13; Gal 3:27). The Holy Spirit is our guide to Christ (1 Cor 6:17), and in the Spirit we receive sonship with God (Gal 3:6).

The Holy Spirit is the foundation of spiritual life and of the unity of love within the Church (Titus 3:4-5; 1 Cor 12:13). As the divine unction, the seal of the Holy Spirit animates the whole body of Christ (1 Jn 2:20, 27). By the Holy Spirit Christians have "access to the Father" (Eph 2:18). The gifts of the Spirit are to be used profitably, for the edification of the Church (1 Cor 12:7; 14:12). The life of the Church itself depends on the operation of the Holy Spirit, for it is the Spirit which appoints bishops to oversee the Church (Acts 20:28). It is the Holy Spirit which sanctifies the decisions taken at church Councils, beginning with the council of Jerusalem (Acts 15:28). For as the Spirit of truth, the Holy Spirit teaches the Church "all things" (Jn 14:16, 27).

St John Chrysostom speaks of the relation of love to the gifts of the Holy Spirit:

> Love builds up, unites, makes the faithful cleave to one another, to be fastened and fitted together. If therefore we desire to obtain the benefits of the Spirit, which come from the Head, let us be in unity with each other. For there are two kinds of separation from the Body of the Church: one, when we become cold in love, the other, when we dare to commit actions unworthy of our belonging to the Body. For in either case we cut ourselves off from the fullness of the Church.

And the holy Father continues:

> Nothing will so avail to divide the Church as the love of power. Nothing so provokes God's displeasure as the division of the Church. Even

though we have performed ten thousand glorious acts, if we destroy the fullness of the Church we suffer punishment no less severe than they who mangled Christ's body.[7]

In the words of St Irenaeus, "Where the Church is, there is the Holy Spirit, and the fullness of grace."[8]

As God the Father was the original source of the divine plan of salvation in Christ, so at the end—after He has put all His enemies under His feet and all things are subjected to Him, including the "last enemy" death—Christ will deliver His kingdom to God the Father, that "God may be all in all" (1 Cor 15:24-28). We know that the end will become reality at the second, glorious coming of Christ, who has promised to the righteous the gift of the kingdom which was prepared for them from before the foundation of the world (Mt 25:31-34).

We can summarize as follows:

1. The Church is the one and only fullness of the divine life of the Holy Trinity for the salvation of the world.

2. The Church regarded simply as "a society of people who believe in Jesus Christ," is not a proper understanding. It is true that the human element is an essential part of the Church, constituting the members of the Body of Christ. Yet the Church's human membership alone does not fully and completely reveal the origin, the nature or the fullness of her divine life.

3. The Church has its origin or initiation in the heavenly abode, in accordance with the pre-eternal plan of God the Father. Expressing God's purpose and the pleasure of His will, the Church began its dwelling on earth in the community of the redeemed believers in Jesus Christ, with the goal of imparting to them salvation in the glorious kingdom of God. When God elevated human nature to glory through the Incarnation of our Savior Jesus Christ,

7 St John Chrysostom, *Op. cit.*, Homily 11.
8 St Irenaeus of Lyons, *Against Heresies,* in *The Ante-Nicene Fathers* (Grand Rapids, 1979), 3:24:1.

He also elevated and gave honor to all of us who belong to and constitute the body of Christ, thereby making them "sit in heavenly places in Christ Jesus" (Eph 2:6).

Finally, we may quote the following definition of the Church as the body of Christ that explains her origin, her divine nature, and her ultimate goal:

> The Church is the divine-human organism whose head is Jesus Christ Himself, and which is animated by the Holy Spirit. The Church was founded by our Lord Jesus Christ and is ruled by Him...even in her earthly aspect, which possesses the apostolic succession of hierarchy. The Church embraces all the faithful in heaven and on earth, who are striving for eternal life in blessed unity with the Holy Trinity, and thus in unity with each other.[9]

9   E. Akvilonov, *Tserkov': Nauchnyie opredelenia* (St Petersburg, 1894), 264.

# 7

# Jesus Christ Is the Head and the Savior of the Church

Our Lord and Savior Jesus Christ, having given authority to the disciples "to observe all things which I have commanded you to do," also promised to be with them "until the end of the world" (Mt 28:20). Indeed, Jesus Christ is forever with the Church, for He is the King of His kingdom (Jn 18:36), He is the foundation of His Church (1 Cor 3:11), He is the founder of His Church (Mt 16:18), He is the Head of His Church (Eph 1:22, 4:15), He is the eternal high priest, "holy, undefiled, higher than the heavens," who offered himself once and for all, for the sins of the people (Heb 7:26-27), He is the possessor of the key to His kingdom (Rev 3:7). He is the God of the living, "for all live unto Him" (Lk 20:38), He is the Great or Chief Shepherd of His flock (Heb 13:20; 1 Pet 5:1-4). Thus the divine origin, the divine nature and the divine life of the Church are rooted in Jesus Christ and in His Kingdom.

Jesus Christ is the head and the savior of the body, the Church. He is one with the Church, as "flesh and bones" (Eph 5:23-30), living in one Spirit with her (1 Cor 6:17). He is the sanctifier of the Church through the Holy Spirit, which He sent upon the apostles to be in the Church forever, bearing his spiritual gifts (Jn 14:16-17; Gal 5:22). Divine life flows from Him as head of the Church, to animate, increase and fulfill the body (Col 2:19).

For the faithful the goal of life in the Church is to attain unity of faith, to "come to the knowledge of the Son of God, unto perfect manhood, unto the measure of the stature of the fullness of Christ" (Eph 4:13). In order to achieve this goal, Jesus Christ

Himself gave the means through which to attain salvation. He entrusted to the Church His divine teaching, and He gave authority to the apostles to teach, baptize, and to do all that is necessary for others to obtain salvation (Mt 28:16-20; Eph 4:11-13). He Himself established the sacrament of the Eucharist (Lk 22:19). He granted the apostles authority to "bind and loose" (Jn 20:22-23), to baptize (Mt 28:19), and to "feed" the Church (Acts 20:28; Jn 21:15-17), in order that she "grow into the House of God by the Spirit" (Eph 2:22).

As the "builders of the mysteries of God" (1 Cor 4:1), the apostles were to judge the Church (1 Tim 5:21-22), to keep order (1 Tim 3:15; Titus 1:5), and to teach sound doctrine (Titus 2:1).

Our Lord Jesus Christ himself invisibly holds the rudder of the Church in His hands, animating the Church by His Holy Spirit (Rom 8:9). He is the source of new, divine Life, for He is the "way, the truth and the life" (Jn 14:6). He promised to found his Church (Mt 16:18), which He acquired with his own blood (Acts 20:28).

The inseparable unity of Jesus Christ with His Body, the Church, is explained by Vladimir Soloviev in this way:

> If Jesus Christ is the way, the truth and the life, who eternally and essentially belongs to the Church, then He belongs to her precisely as the way, the truth and the life. Apostolic succession of the hierarchy, which has its foundation in Christ, is the way by which the divine power of Christ is spread, thereby animating the whole body of the Church. The divine dogma that confesses Jesus Christ to be perfect God and perfect Man is the truth. And the holy sacraments are the foundation and principle of divine life within us. Thus, in the Church's hierarchy Christ himself is present as the way. In the confession of faith He is present as the truth. And in the sacraments, He becomes the source of Life. The unity of these three corresponds to the Kingdom of God, whose ruler is our Lord Jesus Christ.[1]

In perfect unity with her head, Jesus Christ, the earthly Church exists in the world with a definite, visible structure and

1    Vladimir Soloviov, *Dukhovnye osnovy zhizni* (New York, 1958), 108.

organization, including the hierarchy, the holy sacraments, and all other external forms of life. She is invisibly ruled, animated, sanctified and blessed by her true head, through the divine power and life of the Holy Spirit. Thus the true life of the Church and its essential qualities are rooted in and defined by the divine nature and divine life of Jesus Christ, who is her head and savior.

organization, including the hierarchy, the holy sacraments, and all other external forms of life. She is invisibly ruled, animated, sanctified and blessed by her true head, through the divine power and life of the Holy Spirit. Thus the true life of the Church and its essential qualities are rooted in and defined by the divine nature and divine life of Jesus Christ, who is her head and savior.

# 8

# The Essential Qualities of the Church

### "I believe...in one holy, catholic, and apostolic Church"

In the preceding chapters we dealt with subjects regarding the divine origin and the divine nature of the Church. In this present chapter we want to speak of the *qualities* of the Church; qualities that reflect the essence of the Church and that differentiate the Church from any other earthly society.

As the Orthodox Church teaches us, and the Holy Scriptures confirm, the Church as the Body of Christ is organically united with her head. Thereby, she is able to participate fully in the essential qualities that characterize her head. The Church is one, for she rests upon the one cornerstone (Eph 2:20). She is holy, for the Church is constantly being built into a holy temple by the Spirit (Eph 2:21-22). The Church is catholic, for she is the fullness of Christ, embracing all nations and all times (Eph 2:14, 20). And the Church is apostolic, since she is built on the holy apostles (Eph 2:20).

These outstanding qualities of the Church may be qualified as *essential* qualities, insofar as they derive from, flow from, and represent the essence of the Church with which they are organically united. The Church in her essence cannot exist without these essential qualities, just as these qualities cannot exist apart from the Church. The Church in its inner nature is described by key adjectives that reveal her essential qualities: one, holy, catholic and apostolic.

## *The Church is One*

Oneness is the most important quality of the Church. Oneness, in fact, is of her very essence. Without it, the Church could not exist. The Church is not only numerically one. She is unique, possessing the fullness of one head, one faith, one baptism, and one divine life of the Holy Trinity (Eph 4:4-6). Oneness is the essence of the Church, just as the Son is one with the Father (Jn 17:21, 23) through the Holy Spirit (1 Jn 4:13).

The Church is one in her origin and foundation. She constitutes one body, of whom Jesus Christ is the founder, the foundation and the head (1 Cor 3:11; Eph 1:23; 2:20; Mt 16:18). The Church unites all her earthly and heavenly members in the oneness of divine life in Christ and the Holy Spirit. For Christ, being the true life, granted this life to his followers by sending the Holy Spirit upon them. Through the indwelling power of the Spirit, Christ unites all things in himself, as the head of the Church (Jn 17:23; Eph 1:22-23).

To express the character of the one Church, Jesus Christ Himself called the Church His "kingdom" over which He holds "kingship" (Jn 18:36; cf. Mt 16:18). The Church is "one body and one spirit" (Eph 4:4; 1 Cor 12:12). She is one body, whose head, Jesus Christ, reigns over one flock (Jn 10:16). She is one vine (Jn 15:1-6), whose branches or members are called, in hope of salvation, to be "holy and undefiled before God in love" (Eph 1:4).

The Church was one at the time of the apostles, comprising a "little flock" of one hundred and twenty members in a perfect unity, possessing the divine "power of Christ" (2 Cor 12:9). And the Church remains one down to our present day, not only "inwardly" in faith and life, but also "outwardly," in that she possesses the canonical structure and apostolic succession of hierarchy (Eph 4:11-13; 1 Cor 12:28; Acts 20:28).

Often in the past, and even in present times, the Church suffered pain and anguish, being rent apart by heretics, schismatics, and generally by human pride and ignorance. She suffered and continues to suffer from those who "speak on their own authority and seek their own glory" (cf. Jn 7:18). Some of her members separate themselves from the body because they are not a "hand" or other specific organ, playing a desired role in that body (1 Cor 12:15). Thus they revolt against the foundation, order and authority of the Church. Then, too, there are many persons who do not live by the life of the Church, by the breath of the Spirit, and who therefore do not recognize the truth that the body must be "fitly joined together in love" (Eph 4:16), to grow into the fullness of Christ (Eph 1:23). Instead, these people regard the Church as something accidental, as a place where they can satisfy their personal ambitions, desires, or even their careers. In the eyes of the Church, individual, personal "wisdom" is nothing other than "foolishness" (1 Cor 1:21-23). For no matter how long these people might exist in the Church, studying and learning, they are "never able to come to the knowledge of truth" (2 Tim 3:7).

The Church is one because she was granted and she possesses one divine truth, which all the faithful must accept with humility and steadfastness as the doctrine of Christ (Jn 7:16). But often intellectual opposition to the true faith or dogma separates a person from the Church as a heretic. In other cases, opposition by the human will to the authority of the Church leads to people separating themselves from her as schismatics. Both of these actions—heresy and schism—are usually rooted in human pride. Both are condemned by the Church, for they stand in direct opposition to the essential quality of the Church's oneness.

According to St Basil the Great, "He who separates himself from the Church walks neither by love nor by the commandments of Christ" (Letter 66). St Basil knows of the existence in his time of "heretics, schismatics and unlawful assemblies." Heretics are those who "alienate themselves from the Church in matters relating to the actual, true faith. Schismatics are those who separate themselves for some ecclesiastical reason and over questions capable of mutual solution. Unlawful assembly refers to gatherings held by disobedient priests or bishops, or by uninformed lay people" (Canon 1). According to St Basil, "pride and exaltation, self-sufficiency and self importance" that are rooted in the human mind, are responsible for the various divisions within the Church (Letters 215, 239).

The great saint offers us one excellent piece of advice: "Indeed, it would be monstrous to feel pleasure in the schisms and divisions of the Church, and not to consider that the greatest good consists in the knitting together of the members of the body of Christ" (Letter 94).[1]

## *The Church is Holy*

The holiness of the Church, as one body and one spirit, goes hand in hand with the oneness of the Church, for both of these qualities are rooted in the divine nature and divine life of the Holy Trinity. This holiness proceeds from the head of the Church, Jesus Christ, who unites the faithful with the Father by the Holy Spirit (Jn 15:1).

The Church is holy because "the root is holy, and so are the branches" (Rom 11:16). The high priest of the Church is Himself "holy and undefiled" (Heb 7:26), and the Holy Spirit dwells within the Church with his holy gifts (Rom 8:14-16), that she might grow into "the holy temple in the Lord" (Eph 2:21).

The Church is holy, for she is sanctified by Jesus Christ, who has "purchased her with His own blood" (Acts 20:28). For "Christ also loved the Church, and gave Himself for her, that He might

---

1  St Basil, "Letters and Select Works," in *A Select Library of Nicene and Post-Nicene Fathers of the Christian Church*, (Grand Rapids, 1957).

sanctify and cleanse her, not having spot or wrinkle, to be holy and without blemish" (Eph 5:25-27). It is He "who gave himself for us, that He might redeem us, and purify unto Himself a peculiar people, zealous of good works" (Titus 2:14), "to present you holy and blameless, and above reproach in His sight" (Col 1:22).

Holiness of life must become the goal of every Orthodox Christian. "As He who called you is holy, you also must be holy in all your conduct" (1 Pet 1:15). We are to be "perfect, as the Father in heaven is perfect" (Mt 5:48), "holy and undefiled before God" (Eph 1:4).

The entire Church and every faithful member constitutes the holy temple of the Holy Spirit. "The Spirit of God dwells in you" (1 Cor 3:16-17), to make of us "the temple of the living God" (2 Cor 6:16). It is in the life of this temple, the Church, that "the love of God is poured out into our hearts by the Holy Spirit" given to us (Rom 5:5).

All holiness and sanctification in the Church proceeds from the head of the Church. Jesus Christ Himself established the apostolic hierarchy of the Church, with the purpose of "perfecting the saints" (Eph 4:12). He gave us His most sacred teachings to sanctify us through the truth (Jn 17:19), to sanctify the faithful by means of the sacraments (Eph 5:26), and to preserve the purity and sanctity of the Gospel of Christ (Gal 1:7-9). The faithful are sanctified by the holiness of the Church. And the Church, having her source of holiness in our Lord Jesus Christ, is never defiled by the sins of her members, but remains always pure and infallible. In the words St Augustine addressed against the Donatists: "Jesus Christ is the principle, the source and the head of all Christian life in the Church...in consequence of its origin, this life can have nothing in common with the sins of the faithful or of their bishops."[2]

Jesus Christ came to call sinners to repentance (Mt 9:13). The holiness of the Church does not depend on her membership,

2  Mersch, *The Whole Christ*, 403.

whose ideal is to be "holy and undefiled" (Eph 1:4), for the ideal is always more full and complete than the reality. In the Church, elements of good and evil live together, for in the Church there are not only vessels of "gold and silver, but also of wood and of earth" (2 Tim 2:20). As with the net containing different kinds of fishes, or the field where wheat and tares grow together, the harvesting and separating of them will be accomplished by God at the end of the world (Mt 13:47-48, 24-30, 36-43).

Meanwhile, "the Lord knows those who are his" (2 Tim 2:19), and false prophets will be known by their fruits, since "the corrupt tree brings forth evil fruit" (Mt 7:15-17). On the other hand, the quest for "purity of heart" and other virtues commanded by Christ charts the way toward moral perfection and salvation in the Kingdom of God (Mt 5:3-12; Lk 6:20-23). The Orthodox Church knows that multitudes of canonized saints have acquired such virtues. They have become members of the heavenly Church, and they now stand before the throne of God (Rev 7:9).

No other essential quality of the Church was so severely assaulted by heretics as holiness, culminating in the heresy of the Donatists during the fourth and fifth centuries. In brief, the Donatists taught that the holiness of the sacraments depended on the personal qualities of the bishop who performed them. If Donatists found a bishop to be even allegedly "unworthy," they considered the sacraments to be "invalid." Thus they undermined the very holiness of the Church herself, for they made that holiness contingent on the personal moral quality of those who performed the sacraments.

Knowing that the holiness of the Church lies uniquely in Jesus Christ and the Holy Spirit, St Augustine categorically rejected the Donatist teaching. He explained that the "holiness of the sacraments" belongs to the Church herself, and not to any particular individual. Members of the hierarchy are empowered by the Church to celebrate the sacraments. But it is the Church that possesses divine grace and the gifts of sanctification, independently of the moral qualities of her servants. According to St. Augustine, the holiness of the Church lies precisely in the divine grace and power of Jesus Christ and the Holy Spirit, expressed in and through the Church's sacraments.[3]

To conclude this section, we refer to the words of St John of Kronstadt concerning the holiness of the Church:

> Everything with which the Church is feeding us is the truth, as the breath and teaching of the Holy Spirit. Thus the Church is a true paradise on earth. I express my deepest gratitude and thanks to our all-holy, all-blessed and all-wise Mother, the Church of God, for sanctifying and preparing me to become a heavenly citizen here on earth. I pay my gratitude to the Church for prayers, services, sacraments and fasting, through which I receive peace and joy, together with spiritual and physical health. I offer praise to our pure and undefiled Mother, the Church of God, who enlightens me by the heavenly Truth and leads me to eternal life and blessedness.[4]

Through the holiness of the Church, which is the divine power and the divine life that proceed from the head and quicken the whole Body, we are called to be "a holy nation" (1 Pet 2:9), having our hearts unblemished in "holiness before God" (1 Thess 3:13). Thus, we can become like those whom St Paul addressed in his letter to the Romans (6:22): "Now that you have been set free from sin and have become servants of God, the return you receive is holiness, and its end, everlasting life."

## The Church is Catholic

The Church in her essence is Catholic (full, universal, conciliar, *sobornaia*). She is beyond time and space. She embraces all nations, races, genders. She is the fullness of Christ, in whom heaven and earth are united (Eph 1:20-23). The Church embraces the world, where the good seeds are planted by Jesus Christ

---

3  V. Troitskii, *Ocherki iz istorii dogmata o Tserkvi* (Moscow, 1913), 518-544.
4  St John of Kronstadt, *Moia zhizn' vo Khriste* (Ithica, 1894), vol. 2, 17, 43, 70.

(Mt 12:37, 28). Our Lord Jesus became incarnate in order to save the world as a whole (Jn 3:16-17). He is the light of the world (Jn 8:12); He is the world's life and light (Jn 1:4). The gospel of Christ must be preached to all nations (Mk 16:15; 13:10), that is, to the entire inhabited earth (Mt 28:19), even to its very ends (Acts 1:8). The Church will last forever, for the Holy Spirit will abide in her forever (Jn 14:16). Thus the catholicity of the Church is an essential quality that derives from the eternal Kingdom of Christ.

St Cyril of Jerusalem gives two meanings for the term catholicity. Defining the word "ecclesia" as the "gathering together" or "assembly of all men," he states:

> The Church is called catholic, because it extends over all the world, from one end of the earth to the other, and because it teaches the fullness of universal doctrines, subjecting the whole of the human race to righteousness and possessing all spiritual gifts (*Catechetical Lectures* 18:3-4).[5]

We can say that in the catholic Church there is no difference of nationalities, countries or genders, but there all persons constitute "one new man" in the body of Christ, being "fellow citizens with the saints in the household of God" (Eph 2:15, 19). Catholicity is not to be understood merely as a geographic concept, for since the time of its inception the Church was not only one and holy; it was also catholic. And this catholicity expressed the inner quality of the Church characterized by the fullness and unity of the living organism which is the body of Christ.

This aspect of catholicity is described most beautifully and simply by St Ignatius of Antioch. He describes the catholic Church [*ekklesia katholiki*] in these terms: "Where the Bishop is, let there also be the whole people; just as where Jesus Christ is, there is the catholic Church."[6]

---

5   See in Schaff, Phillip and Henry Wage (editors), *The Nicene and Post-Nicene Fathers* (Grand Rapids, MI, 1971), vol. 7, 4.

6   See "The Epistle to the Smyrneans," in Roberts, *The Ante-Nicene Fathers* (Grand Rapids, MI, 1963), vol. 1, 86.

From this perspective, every local church in the world, headed by a canonically ordained bishop, is catholic. Its identity is grounded in sacramental fullness, expressed through faith and holiness, and especially through the eucharist celebrated by the bishop.

Father Georges Florovsky summarizes for us the deepest meaning of the Church's catholicity:

> The Church is Catholic, not only because it is an all-embracing entity, not only because it unites all its members, all local churches, but because it is Catholic in every aspect: in its smallest part and in every act and event of its life. The very nature of the Church is Catholic; the very web of the Church's Body is Catholic. The Church is Catholic because it is one Body of Christ. It is union in Christ and oneness of the Holy Spirit, and this unity and oneness represents the highest degree of wholeness and fullness. The measure of Catholic unity is that 'of one heart and of one soul' (Acts 4:32). Where this is not the case, the life of the Church is limited and restricted. The ontological blending of persons is, and must be, accomplished in oneness with the Body of the Church. They cease to be exclusive and impenetrable. The cold separation into 'mine' and 'thine' disappears.

Explaining further the meaning of Catholicity, Father Georges speaks of another aspect: the meaning of "sobornost'," the perfect, inner unity of the living organism of the whole Body of Christ. The Church catholic is also conciliar [*sobornaia*], for:

> The Church is a unity not only in the sense that it is one and unique; it is a unity striving to reunite a separated and divided mankind. This kind of unity constitutes the "sobornost'" or catholicity of the Church.[7]

The principle of "sobornost'" lies in the unity of essence and the unity of life shared by the three persons of the Holy Trinity who constitute one Divine Being. So also the body of the Church is one in essence, consisting of the variety in plurality of its members. It is the unity of the divine life of Christ and the Holy Spirit, the life that permeates the whole body of the Church. This life expresses the reality of the gathering together of all the faithful, not

---

7  Rev. G.V. Florovsky, "Sobornost': the Catholicity of the Church," in *The Church of God* (London, 1934), 58-60.

only as a visible unity in a particular place, but in a much deeper sense, as a living "unity in variety" or "oneness in multiplicity." For the truth is entrusted to the whole Church in its essential unity, by the love of our Lord Jesus Christ. And that truth is preserved in the Church by the Holy Spirit.[8]

This idea that the divine truth is preserved by the whole Church is expressed by the Encyclical Message of the Eastern Patriarchs of 1848, which says that "the people [*laos*] of the Body of the Church are the guardians of piety." This is grounded in the affirmation of John 17:19, "For their sake I sanctify myself, that they also might be sanctified in the Truth."

Father Sergei Bulgakov offers this explanation of the meaning of sobornost' or conciliarity:

> The word is derived from the verb *sobirat'*, to gather together, to assemble. From this comes the word "Sobor," meaning either Council; or Cathedral. The Slavic text of the Nicean Creed translated the Greek word Katholiki into the adjective Sobornaia. To believe in the Sobornaia Church, is to believe in the Catholic Universal Church that assembles and unites, in opposition to the purely monarchical ecclesiology.[9]

Thus the Church is *sobornaia*, (conciliar, catholic, universal) living in harmonious unity of the divine life in Jesus Christ for the purpose of preserving, guarding, and, if necessary, defending the Orthodox Faith with the help of the Holy Spirit. It is the Church of the conciliar principle established by the apostles, the Church of the Ecumenical Councils, and the Church councils of the present day, where the sobornost' is expressed in the living conciliar unity of all.

> The Sobor (Council) is the expression of the common concern for the Church of all her members, as the "royal priesthood," and the expression also of the Hierarchical structure. This is "sobornost'" (conciliarity) as it is understood to be in the Orthodox Church. It is co-

---

8   Aleksei Khomiakov, *Izbrannye Sochineniia* (New York, 1955), 211, 279, 256.
9   Sergius Bulgakov, *The Orthodox Church* (London, 1935), 74, 75.

operation of love and Spirit in which each member of the Church is given possibility to express the views to enrich other with his experience, to teach and to be taught, to give and to receive God gifts for the good of the whole Church. While the hierarchy, as the apostolic successors, are the guardians and interpreters of truth, being the voice of the Church.[10]

## The Church is Apostolic

The Church is apostolic, built upon the foundation of the apostles and prophets, Jesus Christ Himself, being the cornerstone (Eph 2:20). Apostolicity belongs to the essence, the very nature, of the Church. Depicted as the "bride," the spouse of the Lamb, the Church is also known as "the great city, the holy Jerusalem, descending out of heaven from God" (Rev 21:9-10). The wall of the city is constructed on twelve foundations, and in them are the names of the twelve apostles of the Lamb (Rev 21:14). The holy city, therefore, is one with the apostolic Church.

Jesus entrusted His apostles with the authority to continue in the world his work of salvation. They accomplished this mission by teaching the true faith, by performing the sacraments, and by governing the life of the Church through the grace and power of the Holy Spirit. The gifts of the Spirit are preserved in the Church through the apostolic succession of the hierarchy, to perform the works of ministry needed to build up the body of Christ (Eph 4:12).

Apostolicity completes and fulfills other essential qualities of the Church. Through the apostles, the Church carried the work of salvation into the world. Without this activity, Christianity would have been reduced to some form of theoretical knowledge, with no power to save. It is the work of the apostles that transforms the historical facts of Christ's life, death and resurrection into a genuine *mission* to the world. It is they who bring the new

10 Alexander Schmemann, "The Church is Hierarchical," in *The Report to the All-American Council*, (Archives, OCA, 1963).

life of the Holy Trinity into the hearts of people, in order that they personally receive the new faith. Indeed, "As Thou hast sent me into the world, so have I also sent them into the world," to bring life-giving truth to those people who shall believe in Jesus Christ through the word of the apostles (Jn 17:18-20). Thereby all might become one flock with one shepherd (Jn 10:16).

All that Christ received from the Father He made known to the apostles (Jn 15:15). He chose and ordained them so that they would bear the fruit of their labor. Thus the Church received from the apostles the holy scriptures, containing the true doctrines of the faith, together with the life-giving sacraments, the canonical structure of the Church, and the apostolic succession of the hierarchy. The apostles were the first to confess Jesus Christ to be the "Son of the living God" (Mt 16:16), and they were the first to establish the apostolic Church, from which the Church grew into one, holy, catholic orthodox Church.

The apostolic succession of the hierarchy is the unbroken continuity of authority within the Church, originating with Jesus Christ, passing to the apostles, and continuing to the present times by the laying on of hands of bishops. The Church is apostolic, because the root and fundamental source of her entire hierarchical structure lies in the apostles themselves.

The essence of this hierarchical principle has been described in this way:

> The hierarchical principle belongs to the nature of the Church. It is a necessary requirement for the organization of the Church, which is the religious society founded according to the principles and commandments of Christ. At its most basic level, the Hierarchical Principle is directly founded by God."[11]

To this description we can add the following: God the Father sends His Beloved Son to earth for the salvation of mankind. Jesus

---

11  N.A. Zaozerskii, "Ierarkhicheskii printsip v tserkovnoi organizatsii" in *Bogoslovskii Vestnik* (1911), 1:84.

Christ, receiving authority from the Father, founded His Church as a divine-human society. He then passed His authority on to His apostles, whom He Himself chose and to whom He gave the command to continue His work for the salvation of the world, a work accomplished in the power of the Holy Spirit. The apostles in turn passed this authority in the Church to their successors, the bishops, through the special sacrament of ordination with the laying on of hands. The bishops, in their turn, passed on this authority to other bishops who were their successors. By this process, the principle of the apostolic succession of hierarchy is preserved within the Church up to the present day.

Like the foundation of the Church itself, the hierarchical principle is revealed to be the work of the Holy Trinity. It is a work of divine origin: God the Father sends God the Son, who, through His incarnation, performs the work of salvation. God the Holy Spirit subsequently descends to fulfill the work of the divine Son through the apostles and their successors.

The hierarchical principle is thus the source of divine life within the Church. It is a principle of divine origin, originating with the authority of the Father transmitted to the Son, and given by the Son through the Holy Spirit to the apostles and their successors, for the work of mankind's salvation accomplished in the Church. Recognizing the authority of the apostolic succession of hierarchy, we affirm that the Church possesses the authority of Jesus Christ Himself.

The Church is apostolic, because the true faith came to us from the apostles. It is important to keep the words and writings of the apostles (2 Thess 2:15) and not pay attention to the heretics (Titus 3:10). The truth of the apostolic teaching must be preserved (Gal 1:8). It must be accepted (cf. 2 Tim 4:14-15) and taught to others (2 Tim 2:2-3).

Apostolic authority within the Church does not belong to any individual, including any bishop. It belongs to the whole unity of bishops, acting in harmony and conciliar unity (Apostolic Canon 34). That authority is given by the "voice of the Church," whose purpose is to serve the body of Christ (Eph 4:12).

To conclude this chapter, we may note the following points. Our Lord Jesus Christ granted His divine truth and life, not to any individual member of His body, but to the whole Church acting in unity. This unity is a unity in love, animated and preserved by the life that proceeds from the head to the body (Eph 4:2-6; Col 2:19). The goal of this spiritual unity that marks the life of the Church is to grow to the "measure and stature of the fullness of Christ" (Eph 4:13).

The Church as the one divine-human organism that constitutes the body of Christ (Eph 4:14) is first revealed to be the inner spiritual unity of human beings with Jesus Christ. Thus Jesus can speak of the "kingdom of God within you" (Lk 17:21), declaring that it is "not of this world" (Jn 18:36).

This same body of Christ, as the divinely instituted community of the faithful on earth (Mt 16:18; 18:20), is the Church, existing and acting in the world. There she fulfills her task and responsibility before God, preserving the unity and holiness of her divine life as the gift of the Holy Trinity. There she safeguards and protects the teaching of Jesus Christ and passes His truth, the truth of faith, to future generations. There, too, she preserves the gifts of divine grace in the form of sacraments. All this she does through the apostolic succession of hierarchy, for the moral perfection and salvation of the faithful in the kingdom of God.

# 9

# The Divine Authority of the Church

**"...the church of the Living God, the pillar and
foundation of the truth" (1 Tim 3:15)**

The good news of our Lord and Savior Jesus Christ is summed up
in the command, "Repent, for the Kingdom of Heaven is at
hand!" (Mt 4:17). Indeed, with the appearance of the incarnate
Son of God on earth, together with His teaching activity and the
witness of His life, the Church which He came to establish became a reality.

The Church of Christ is the kingdom of God, for she has inherited the divine fullness of her founder and head, and she has
received the Holy Spirit, who forever lives within her to animate
and rule her life. The Church is the kingdom of God because of
the goal and destiny which is hers to bring all humans into the
heavenly abode of God, persons who can even now participate in
the heavenly divine life of the Church.

This heavenly kingdom which is the Church—beginning with
the time at which Jesus Christ, God's eternal Son, became incarnate—was established as a full reality after the completion of Jesus'
public ministry. It was founded by Jesus Himself, upon his teaching,
life, suffering, death, resurrection, and ascension to heaven in glory.
Jesus completed the founding of his Church on earth by sending his
Holy Spirit upon his apostles, thereby creating a kingdom of "righteousness, peace and joy in the Holy Spirit" (Rom 14:17).

As the kingdom of God, the Church received from her head
the fullness of divine authority on earth. The Church thus possesses authority to open or close the heavens (Mt 16:19); author-

ity to bind and to loose the sins of men (Mt 18:18; Jn 20:22-23); authority to regenerate and to save the whole world (Jn 3:3, 16). As the body of Christ, the living organism animated by the Holy Spirit, the Church is infallible.

From her head and ruler, Jesus Christ, the Church received authority to govern, to sanctify, to renew, to regenerate, and to purify the faithful through the holy sacraments. Thereby the Church offers the faithful the possibility to attain sonship to God, by uniting them to the divine nature in the mystery of communion in the Body and Blood of the Son of God. And she can do so, because she is governed by the authority of the Holy Spirit that comes to visible expression in the authority of the hierarchy.

Having Jesus Christ as her head, and participating in his divine nature, the Church also inherits Christ's divine authority, for "Where I am, there you may be also" (Jn 14:3). Having the Spirit of God, the Church also possesses the "mind of Christ" (1 Cor 2:12, 16), and thus she is infallible by her very nature. The *Encyclical Message of the Orthodox Patriarchs* of 1723 (no. 2) asserts specifically that the Church is infallible: "The Church cannot ever err, be deceived, or be wrong in her judgment. For equally with the Holy Scriptures the Church is infallible, and she is forever the same in her nature, as God founded her."[1]

The Church must use her authority not against "flesh and blood, but against the rulers of the darkness of this world, against spiritual wickedness" (Eph 6:12). The Church is the final judge in worldly matters (Mt 18:17), but she is also the merciful and loving mother, who forgives her children "seventy times seven" (Mt 18:22).

The Church has a great responsibility before God, to protect and preserve the truth entrusted into her hands. For just as those who despised the law of Moses died without mercy, so those members of the Church will receive even worse punishment "who

---

1   *Encyclical Messages of the Orthodox Patriarchs* (1723), no. 2.

trampled underfoot the Son of God," for "it is a dreadful thing to fall into the hands of the living God" (Heb 10:28-31).

Initiated by God the Father, revealed by the Son of God, Jesus Christ, preserved by the Holy Spirit since Pentecost, the truth was entrusted to the apostles and their successors in the Church for the benefit of all and for all times. The source and foundation of the authority of the Church is the will of the Father, who gave authority to His Son (Mt 28:18; Lk 10:16), and who sent upon the apostles and upon the Church as a whole the "Spirit of Truth" (Jn 14:16-17; 15:26; 16:13). Thus from her inception the Church of Christ possesses authority characterized by a divine origin, a divine foundation, and a divine life and truth in unity and love. Possessing these divine and eternal qualities, the Church of the present times is essentially identical to the Church of the first century; and she will remain such to the end of the world, according to the promise of her founder (Mt 16:18; 28:20).

The divine authority of the Church is founded in our Savior Jesus Christ: in His divine truth and teaching, his divine life and love, his wisdom and knowledge, his commandments to the apostles, and his Holy Spirit, by whom the fullness of divine gifts was passed to the Church, making it possible for her members to become participants in the divine nature (Eph 3:10; Col 2:3; 2 Pet 1:4). In order to be truly "authoritative," the Church must "gather with Christ" (Lk 11:23). This means that human effort is necessary, together with the work of the Holy Spirit, in order to express the whole truth within the Church.

The *Encyclical Message of the Orthodox Patriarchs of 1848* confirms that "Neither patriarchs nor councils could bring innovations, because the preserver of piety and faith is the whole body of the Church, that is, the faithful people, who always wish to preserve the faith unchangeable and in accordance with the teaching of the Fathers."[2]

2   Ibid., (1848), no. 17.

The fullness of Christ is communicated to the Church, for "the Church is the fullness of Him that fills all in all" (Eph 1:22-23). The Church represents Christ in the world, by possessing his life and not simply by seeking him. The head completes the body, and the body completes the head. Thus the body, the Church, organically united with its head, naturally becomes the inheritor and possessor of the divine qualities of its head: "I am the way, the truth and the life" (Jn 14:6).

Jesus Christ is the apostle and high priest (Heb 3:1), invisibly ruling the Church. He is "the same yesterday and today and forever" (Heb 13:8), and so is his infallible Church, for, as St Irenaeus has said, "Where the Church is, there is the Spirit of God, and where the Spirit of God is, there is the Church and every grace; and the Spirit is Truth."[3] It is this Spirit of Christ who animates and constitutes the inner essence of the body of Christ.

The Church occupies a central place in all aspects of our knowledge of God. For she is the source, the guardian, the interpreter, the teacher and the authority of everything that is related to the question of man's salvation, together with his moral and spiritual life. In reality, the Church is the point from which there begins, in which there is preserved, and to which return the entire body of Christian truth and knowledge, including the Holy Scriptures and Holy Tradition.

This central position of the Church as the preserver and guardian of truth is clearly expressed in the Holy Scriptures. There the Church is declared to be "the pillar and foundation of the truth" (1 Tim 3:15). The same idea is expressed in the affirmation that the Church is "the fullness of Christ" (Eph 1:23), commissioned to continue His work in the world while being preserved "holy and without blemish" (Eph 5:27).

---

3   St Irenaeus, *Against Heresies*, in *The Ante-Nicene Fathers: Translations of the Writings of the Fathers down to AD325*, (Grand Rapids, 1979), 3:24.1.

The Church, therefore, is indeed infallible, being the first and last source of the knowledge of God:

> We believe that the Holy Spirit is the One who teaches the Catholic Church, for He is the true Comforter, whom Jesus Christ has sent from the Father to teach truth and expel darkness from the human mind. Therefore we are not only convinced but without doubt confess as the firm truth, that the Universal Church cannot sin, err, or pronounce a lie instead of truth. For the Holy Spirit being always active through his servants (fathers and teachers) of the Church preserves the Church from any heresy, error or delusion.[4]

Our Lord Jesus Christ entrusted His "way, truth and life," not to one particular person, but to the assembly of the apostles, and through them to the whole Church. Thereby, under the leadership of the hierarchy, the Church became the depository and guardian of truth, realizing her authority in the name of Jesus Christ and the Holy Spirit.

St Irenaeus of Lyons, in his writing against heresies, explained most excellently the position of the Church as the depository of truth, as the interpreter of the Holy Scriptures and Holy Tradition, and as the guardian and protector of truth. The truth is to be found, he declared, nowhere else but in the Catholic Church, the sole depository of the apostolic faith:

> Since the apostles deposited into the treasury of the Church all things pertaining to the truth, so now every man can draw from the Church the water of life, for the Church is the entrance into life.[5]

The apostles, he affirms, handed down the truth through the living word of Tradition to those to whom they committed the Church.

St Irenaeus further teaches that the Church is the Depository of Truth through the Apostolic Succession of Hierarchy:

---

4  *Encyclical Messages of the Orthodox Patriarchs* (1723), no. 12.
5  *Op. cit.*, St Irenaeus, *Against Heresies*, 3:4.1.

The blessed apostles, having founded and built up the Church, committed her into the hands of the episcopate (here he names Linus as the
first bishop of Rome). In this order and by this succession, the ecclesiastical tradition from the apostles, and teaching of truth, have come
down to us. And this is most abundant proof that there is one and the
same vivifying faith, which was preserved in the Church from the apostles until now, and handed down in truth.[6]

And although the Church is scattered all over the world, St
Irenaeus continues, and is planted in countries using many different languages, she remains the preserver of truth:

The Church received from the apostles and their successors the true
faith. She carefully preserves the truth, as if occupying one house, believing as one soul and one heart, proclaiming the truth as one mind.
And the Church, planted all over the world, is one. Just as the sun,
God's creation, is one and the same throughout the world, so also the
teaching of the truth shines everywhere and enlightens all men who are
willing to come to the knowledge of the truth. Nor will anyone in authority (rulers) in the Church, however highly gifted he may be, teach
doctrines different from these.[7]

If anyone wants to learn the true faith, he can find the apostolic tradition in every Church founded by the apostles, where
that tradition is preserved by successor-bishops, to whom the
apostles entrusted their teaching and responsibility for the
Church. For with the apostolic succession, the episcopate has received from God "the certain gift of truth."[8]

"The pillar and the foundation" of the Church is the Gospel and
the Spirit of life, St Irenaeus affirms. The Church is the interpreter of
truth, just as she is the road that leads to salvation. "Undoubtedly,
the teaching of the Church is true and steadfast. In the Church one
and the same way of salvation is shown to people throughout the
whole world. For to the Church is entrusted the light of God and
therefore the wisdom of God, by which means she saves all men."

6   Ibid., 3:3.3.
7   Ibid., 1:10.1, 2.
8   Ibid., 3:3.1; 4:26.2.

The faithful should avoid heretical teaching, in order not to be injured by it. They should "flee to the Church, and be brought up in her bosom, and be nourished with the Lord's Scriptures. For the Church has been planted as paradise in this world.... For the Holy Spirit, dwelling in man, becomes the head of man, for through Him (the Spirit) we see, and hear and speak."[9]

This conviction that the Church is truly the "pillar and foundation of truth," and that she is the path to salvation, was embraced by the fathers of the second ecumenical council (381), who adopted the *Symbol of Faith* of the Orthodox Church. Although this council placed the Church as the ninth article of faith, we must nevertheless remember that it was the Church herself that called the Council to act in her name as the guardian and teacher of truth.

Although the whole Church is the custodian of truth, it is not the whole Church "de facto" that is called to be the Church's voice. Who does express the voice of the Church? How was this question resolved in the early centuries? The founder of the Church Himself, Jesus Christ, gave us the answer by choosing and commissioning the apostles to be His representatives in the world. Thus the first voice of the Church was that of the apostles, and later their successor-bishops became that voice, expressing truth in the Church. An example is Timothy, who was entrusted by the Paul to guard the truth, to "hold fast the sound words in faith and love in Jesus Christ" (2 Tim 1:12-13). To ensure that the original, true faith of Jesus Christ and the apostles is preserved to the end of the world, the Church possesses the apostolic succession of hierarchy, founded directly by God.

The highest ecclesiastical authority in expressing the true faith of the Orthodox Church is the ecumenical council. Such councils are composed of all bishops of all Orthodox Churches, guided by the Holy Spirit in accordance with the affirmation of the first ap-

9  Ibid., 3:11.8; 5:20.1-2.

ostolic council in Jerusalem: "It seemed good to the Holy Spirit and to us" (Acts 15:28). The decisions of an ecumenical council, however, must be followed by reception by the people, who ratify the truth of those decisions (Acts 15:31).

Thus the Church—as the divine-human society of believers in Christ, the Son of the living God, being invisibly governed by Him and guided by the Holy Spirit, while being visibly governed by the hierarchy—is truly the source, the guardian, and the teacher of all God's truth unto ages of ages.

Having firm assurance from her founder and head, together with the Holy Spirit, that Jesus Christ will be present with the Church until the "end of the world"—and because "the gates of hell shall not prevail against her"—the Church accomplishes her task in the world by revealing the truth of God in manifold, multifaceted ways. As teacher of truth, the Church proclaims:

1. The Church is the source, the guardian and the interpreter of the Holy Scriptures and Holy Tradition, which equal each other in authority: "Brethren, stand fast and hold the traditions which you were taught, whether by word or by our epistle" (2 Thess 2:15; Jn 16:13).

2. The dogmatic theology of the Orthodox Church is the science which, in systematic order, reveals to the world the dogmas or doctrines related to all aspects of God's providence and activity in the world. Dogmatic theology presents the dogmas as the truth of God. Divine in origin, the dogmas are unchangeable, immutable. They are truths formulated and defined by the Church, and therefore they have absolute authority for all members of the Church.

3. Orthodox moral theology is the science which, again in systematic order, explains the teachings relating to the moral life of man, as that life is to be lived in accordance with God's laws and commandments, in harmony with His will. The perfect and absolute example of moral perfection, accordingly, is our Lord Jesus Christ.

Moral theology and dogmatic theology have much in common. They embrace the same subjects: God and man; law and freedom; the virtues of faith, hope and love; questions of life and death. Both disciplines lead to salvation. By studying dogmatic theology, we learn the objective revelation of God's truth, His commandments and His action within the world. Moral theology, on the other hand, teaches about our acceptance of truth and our response to God's will and providence. That response involves accepting and fulfilling the moral commandments of God, as the living path to salvation. Both sciences, dogmatic and moral theology, have as their source and foundation our Lord Jesus Christ. Dogmatic theology knows Him as the creator, savior, redeemer and final judge of mankind. Moral theology knows Jesus Christ as the perfect ideal and example in all aspects of the Christian moral life, through whom we work out our own salvation "with fear and trembling" (Phil 2:12).

Our Lord Jesus Christ is the absolute criterion in the personal and social moral life of every Christian. The Most Holy Theotokos or Mother of God, together with the Saints of the Church, also serves as guiding lights who direct the moral life of the faithful when they find themselves in doubt or confusion concerning particular moral questions.

Moral theology must not be confused with all kinds of moral philosophies, which, unlike the morality of the Orthodox Church, base their teachings on purely human knowledge.

It is important for us to note that the Holy Scriptures tell us of an inner, natural moral law which is innate to the entire human race. This is a law "written on the heart," judged by the conscience which serves as the criterion of human moral activity (Rom 2:14-15). The human conscience, however, can become sinful, unreliable, or even completely dead. The Biblical word speaks of those whose "foolish heart was hardened" (Rom 1:21). When man becomes independent of divine law, he establishes

himself as his own criterion in matters regarding his moral and social actions. By denying God's providence, the world and its life
become secularized. Relativism, pride, self-love, egotism—the
qualities which presently rule the world—are to some extent governed and limited by the laws of states and civil authorities. It is
precisely for this reason that the God of history presented mankind with His positive moral laws: the Law of Moses in the Old
Testament, and the new divine Law of Jesus Christ in the New
Testament (Jn 1:17; Gal 6:2; Heb 1:2).

4. Pastoral theology is the science that deals with questions
pertaining to the Priesthood: its nature, origin, calling, education,
and ordination, together with the threefold service of Jesus
Christ, including teaching, serving the sacred sacraments, and
pastoral care of the faithful. This last emphasizes the practice of
confession and adherence to the moral law of the Church. Pastoral theology includes such subjects as the personal, social and family life of the priest; the matter of the priest's material subsistence;
questions concerning his responsibility toward civil authorities;
and his involvement in charity and in the needs of the world in
general. Pastoral theology demands that authentic spiritual and
moral life begin with the leaders of the Church—bishops, pastors
and teachers—and demands that they not fall under God's con-
demnation for failing to practice what they themselves preach
(Rom 2:8). In fact, the Church's pastors are called to be the first of
all those who bear Christ's Cross in the world.

Pastoral theology is often combined with the science of com-
parative theology, which concerns chiefly the theological differences and problems arising in relations between the Orthodox
Church and other Christian churches, confessions or different
world religions. Those differences and problems include matters
of faith, salvation, authority and the structure of the Church.

5. Liturgical theology addresses the nature, origin, structure
and meaning of the divine sacraments, personal and collective

prayer, church art and music, and in general, everything necessary for the life of sanctification, moral perfection, and salvation within the Church. Church History includes an overview of the liturgical life of the Church as it has developed over the past two thousand years.

6. The Church, having inherited divine authority from her founder to govern and judge (Mt 18:15-18; 2 Cor 10:5-6; Jn 20:21, Acts 20:29), has developed its own distinctive body of Canon Law. This is purely ecclesiastical law, independent of any civil authority. These laws or canons regulate and direct not only the inner spiritual and moral life of the faithful, but, more importantly, these canons protect the existence of the Church in the political, economic and social environment of the contemporary world. They do so by safeguarding and protecting the essential qualities of the Church: oneness, holiness, catholicity, and apostolicity.[10]

The Universal Code of Canons was established by the Sixth Ecumenical Council (Canon 2). We need to remember that the Ecumenical Councils are the supreme dogmatic, canonical and legislative authority for the entire Orthodox Church. All dogmatic and canonical decisions made by Ecumenical Councils are adopted under the guidance of the Holy Spirit (Acts 15:28). They are God-inspired, and all of them must be confirmed by being formally received by the members of the Church.[11] Therefore, all dogmatic definitions of the Councils, and all canons based on Holy Scriptures, which reveal the dogmatic principles of faith and morality, or the succession of hierarchy by which the divine grace of the Holy Spirit is preserved in the Church, are immutable and unchangeable for all times.

However, some canons of historic or disciplinary nature, which were adopted for a certain time and place, are variable and mutable. They can be changed by the same authority of the Church which

10 Sixth Ecumenical Council, Canon 1, Apostolic Canons 34, 61 and others.
11 Seventh Ecumenical Council, Canon 1.

adopted them in the first place. This idea that some disciplinary canons can be changed, and have been, does not in any way weaken the witness of the Church Fathers, who affirm that their activity at the Ecumenical Councils was God-inspired. We need to keep in mind the fact that the Old Testament, in all its fullness, was granted to us by God. Nevertheless, when the time came, the customs and the ritual law of the Old Covenant were canceled. Yet no Orthodox Christian doubts the divinely inspired character of the Old Testament in general.

An analogy can be made with the canonical activity of the Ecumenical Councils. For "because of the demands of history or of local circumstances, the Church, possessing the full authority of God, and not without His help, permits changes in her ecclesiastical discipline, having the good of the Church and the fulfillment of God's plan of salvation as its reason and goal."[12]

For all these gifts of God to His Church, every person must be prepared to answer with faith, as well as spiritual and moral life, as a true member of the Orthodox Church in order to find an answer to the question: "What good things shall I do, that I may have eternal life?" (Mt 19:16).

12  P.P. Ponomorev, *Sviashchennoe predanie, kak istochnik Khristianskogo vedeniia* (Kazan, 1908), 311.

# The Life of the Church

"I am the way, the truth, and the life..." (Jn 14:6)

The Church, as the spiritual Kingdom of God, is the beginning of perfect, all embracing divine life, without earthly limitations. The Church of Christ is the leaven that transforms the world from all evil and imperfection into the divine life of Christ in the Holy Spirit. The faithful can begin to live this life during their earthly existence. To be in communion with Christ, the Holy Spirit, and God the Father means to live within the Church, for the Church—being the pathway that leads to the Kingdom of God—is in complete unity with the Holy Trinity. As a divine-human institution, the Church is the realm in which those who believe in Jesus Christ become participants of His saving acts. In the Church they receive the grace of the Holy Spirit, in order that they might attain holiness of life and spirit (Jn 6:63), and eventually, eternal life in the Kingdom of God. Thus it is in the Church that the way, the truth and the life of salvation in the Kingdom are revealed and actualized.

Divine truth is one. It originates with God the Father, it was revealed in our Lord Jesus Christ, and it is preserved in the Church by the Holy Spirit. Divine truth was preached by the apostles, and it is now being guarded and preserved for the benefit of all and for all times by the bishops, who are the apostles' successors. The criterion of truth is Jesus Christ, who is Himself the Truth and who dwells within the Church to communicate His divine revelation. The final protector of truth from heresies and falsehood is the whole body of faithful members of the Church. Thus, we affirm that all knowledge of God's truth can be found in the Orthodox Church, which lives by the fullness and the mind of Christ. This is confirmed by the *Encyclical Messages of the Orthodox Patriarchs* (1723, no. 2):

> We believe that the Truth of God as taught by the Orthodox Church, and the Truth of God contained in the Holy Scriptures, are one and the same. For the source of Truth in Scripture and in the Church is one and the same, namely the Holy Spirit. Thus we acquire knowledge of God's Truth either from the Scriptures or in the Orthodox Church.[1]

Those who desire to learn God's truth will, in most cases, find that it is easier to do so through the Orthodox Church herself, since for the past two thousand years she has been in actual possession of the objective truth of God through the Holy Scriptures and Tradition. This truth has structured the whole of her life: her theology, her doctrine and sacraments, her experience of spiritual and moral life, her liturgy with its sanctifying services and prayers, her customs, her church art, music and culture, her canonical and hierarchical structure, and all aspects of church life directed toward the regeneration of man's spiritual and physical nature. In short, whoever desires new life and salvation may acquire them in their fullness within Christ's Holy Church.[2]

We know that our Lord Jesus Christ became incarnate and offered Himself to all people, without exception. "He is the expiation for our sins; and not ours only, but also for the sins of the whole world" (1 Jn 2:2). "God our Savior...desires all men to be saved and to come to the knowledge of the Truth" (1 Tim 2:3-4). Nevertheless, these affirmations should not be interpreted to mean that everyone will unquestionably be saved. For it is not enough just to know the objective teaching of Jesus Christ. The entire human race is called to salvation, but only those will be

---

1   *Encyclical Messages of the Orthodox Patriarchs* (1723), no. 2.
2   We often hear the familiar assertion: "Outside of the Church there is no salvation." This formula in fact stipulates *where* salvation is to be found rather than addressing the question of *who* will be saved. It is therefore a positive statement about the Church, rather than a negative.

saved who hear the voice of Him who calls, and then follow Him by submitting to the principles of faith and by leading a life in accordance with His commandments. Although "many are called," Jesus can affirm in his parable that "none of those who were bidden shall taste of my supper" (Lk 14:24), for they have not "obeyed the gospel" (Rom 10:16).

It is clear that salvation depends not only upon knowledge of the objective conditions which are applied to all persons. It also, and most importantly, depends on the personal, subjective and voluntary acceptance of God's commandments concerning faith and life. God cannot save us contrary to our free will or desire. Everyone must seek salvation through a working harmony (synergy) between his own effort and God's grace.

All conditions for salvation are centered in the person of Jesus Christ, in His teaching and life. In Christ, everyone can obtain salvation (2 Tim 2:10). Yet they must "hear with their heart" and be "converted" (Mt 13:15), becoming like "little children," in order to enter the Kingdom of Heaven (Mt 18:3). They must be converted to receive healing (Jn 12:40). This requires that they believe and turn to Jesus Christ (Acts 11:21), and that they repent or convert, doing works of repentance (Acts 26:20), and then the Lord will enlighten them (2 Cor 3:16).

This means that conversion to Christ demands repentance before all else (Mt 4:17; Mk 1:14; Acts 2:38; 2 Pet 3:9; Rom 2:4). Repentance expresses an absolute desire to change the direction of one's life. Christian existence begins with our response to the call to "repent and be converted" (Acts 3:19), and it continues with our striving to find the true road to salvation in Christ through faith.

Faith is the beginning of Christian life. Faith is the firm and perfect conviction that Jesus Christ is the incarnate Son of the living God, and that He alone can save us (Acts 4:12). Such faith is "the substance of things hoped for, and the evidence of things not seen"

(Heb 11:1). Repentance and faith are followed by hope and love, of which love is the greatest gift that never ends (1 Cor 13:8, 13).

By faith the whole inner structure of life becomes grounded in a response of obedience to God and to His laws. The knowledge that there exists One God (Jas 2:19) is innate to mankind. To discover and realize who the true God is, and to have faith in Him, should become the major goal and a labor of love for every person on earth. Christians find the true God in His Word and through His Holy Church. And those who truly know Him, those who are true followers of Christ, will be known by their deeds (Jn 13:25; 17:23).

Thus "if you confess with your mouth the Lord Jesus, and believe in your heart that God has raised Him from the dead, you will be saved. For with the heart one believes unto righteousness, and with the mouth confession is made unto salvation"(Rom 10:9, 10). "Without faith, it is impossible to please Him," for He is the "rewarder of those who diligently seek Him" (Heb 11:6). Such living faith, together with prayer, can be helpful to others as well as to ourselves, by leading them to seek healing and the forgiveness of their sins (Mt 9:1-8). "As the body without the spirit is dead, so faith without works is dead also" (Jas 2:26). Our faith must be living and active: if anyone confesses Christ, Christ will acknowledge him "before the angels of God" (Lk 12:8).

Faith and love must be expressed in Christian life in the form of deeds or works, for "faith without works is dead" (Jas 2:24-26). In order to pursue repentance, faith, hope and love, we need God's help:

"For the grace of God has appeared for the salvation of all men, teaching us that, denying ungodliness and worldly lusts, we should live soberly, righteously and godly lives in this present world, awaiting the blessed hope and the appearance in glory of our great God and Savior Jesus Christ, who gave Himself for us, that He might redeem us from all iniquity, and purify for Himself a people of His own who are zealous for good works" (Titus 2:11-14). All this God has accomplished so that we might be united to Christ to the point that Jesus Christ truly lives in us (cf. Gal 2:20).

Such full and complete devotion to our Lord Jesus Christ would be impossible for a sinful person to attain without the supernatural help and the divine grace of the Holy Spirit. Our faith in Jesus Christ, and our conversion to Him, is impossible without God's help: "No one can come to me unless the Father, who has sent me, draws him" (Jn 6:44), just as no one can call Jesus Christ "except by the Holy Spirit" (1 Cor 12:3), since our faith itself is the fruit of the Holy Spirit (Gal 5:22; 1 Cor 12:9; Rom 12:3). All of Christian life, in fact, depends on the divine help of God acting through the Holy Spirit (Jn 15:3; Rom 8:9-10, 26).

Our conversion to our savior Jesus Christ, together with our growth in the divine grace of the Holy Spirit, is the true path toward our unity with Christ and our life in Him. It is by this unity that we inherit and become participants in the saving life and work of our Lord. This includes our redemption, our becoming a "new creation" (Gal 6:15), and our salvation attained by abiding in Him. But it also obliges us to bear fruit in His name and by His power: "for without me you can do nothing" (Jn 15:4-6). Therefore it is absolutely essential that we be entirely united to Christ, becoming truly one with Him who is the Source of divine, eternal life.

It is also necessary to acquire "the mind of Christ" (1 Cor 2:16), for "if you continue in my work, then you are my disciples indeed" (Jn 8:31; 15:7). In order to live with Christ and in Christ, we must be of one will with Him. This we achieve by accepting God's providence and by full compliance with His commandments, for "he who has my commandments and keeps them, he it is who loves me; and he who loves me will be loved by my Father, and I will love him and manifest myself to him... If a man loves me, he will keep my word, and my Father will love him, and we will come to him and make our home with him" (Jn 14:21, 23).

He who keeps the commandments of Christ "dwells in Him by the Spirit which He has given us" (1 Jn 3:24).

To have the most intimate, inner and mystical union with Christ, we become spiritually and corporally united with Him by communicating in His Body and Blood. Thereby we enter into the Body of Christ, His Church (1 Cor 10:16; 12:27), with the result that "whoever eats my flesh and drinks my blood abides in me, and I in him" (Jn 6:56). This is the pathway to resurrection and eternal life (Jn 6:54), a pathway that gives us access to God the Father only through Jesus Christ, by the Holy Spirit (Eph 2:18).

It is by hearing the Word of God that divine grace opens man's heart and mind to the knowledge of God: "For the Word of God is quick and powerful and sharper than any two-edged sword, piercing even to the dividing of soul and spirit" (Heb 4:12). Faith enters into a person who "has ears to hear," for "faith comes by hearing, and hearing by the Word of God" (Rom 1:17). Thereby, "Christ may dwell in your heart by faith" (Eph 2:17). Subsequently, divine life enters into a person through baptism: "for as many as have been baptized into Christ have put on Christ" (Gal 3:27), in whom dwells "all the fullness of the Godhead bodily" (Col 2:9). Christ imparts His own divine power to the newly baptized person, who is thereby born of God (Jn 1:13). Divine grace, bestowed by the Holy Spirit, enters into the life of the newly baptized person through the sacrament of chrismation. This harkens back to the experience of the early Church: "They laid their hands on them, and they received the Holy Spirit" (Acts 8:15). Through chrismation God anoints us in Christ. He sealed us and gave us the Holy Spirit in our hearts (2 Cor 1:21-22). God's divine life enters the life of the new Christian in the fullest way through the sacrament of the eucharist.

The whole fullness of life in the Church is sacramental, because the Holy Spirit is constantly and uninterruptedly acting in the sacraments. It is by this action that the true, divine nature of the Church is realized.

In baptism, with its appeal to God for "a clear conscience" (1 Pet 3:21), the faithful are united to Christ by water and the Holy Spirit. They "put on Christ," dying with him in his death and being raised with him in his resurrection, in order to walk in "newness of life" (Rom 6:3-4; Gal 3:27). Through baptism a person is initiated into the divine-human life of the Church. The proclamation of the *Symbol of Faith* at the baptismal ceremony is an oath of allegiance to God and the Church.

The new life of conversion begins with "putting off the old man" with his deeds, and "putting on the new man," fashioned in the image of Him who created him in righteousness and holiness (Col 3:9-10; Eph 4:24). Thus in baptism those who "put on Christ" accept both the responsibility and the power to live by the life of Christ, to possess His mind, to desire what He desires, to act as He acts, and to reveal Christ in themselves."[3] In baptism the inner moral structure of man's life is essentially changed.

Chrismation is the sacrament of the "seal" of the Holy Spirit, that seals and anoints us in our hearts (cf. 2 Cor 1:21). We are sealed unto the day of redemption (Eph 4:30). We have an unction from the Holy One (1 Jn 2:20), and we are made members of the royal priesthood and of the family of God.

In the sacraments of repentance (confession) and holy unction, Christians reveal their conscience and their will before God: "If we confess our sins, He is faithful and just, and will forgive our sins and cleanse us from all unrighteousness" (1 Jn 1:9). Repentance is like a second baptism, when a person voluntarily renounces sins and the sinful life, and accepts forgiveness of those confessed sins which were the cause of his separation from God and the Church. Holy unction bestows the help and grace of God in times of illness and suffering, and it is also for the forgiveness of sins (Jas 5:14-15).

3   St Theophan [Feofan], "Commentary on Galatians" in *Tolkovaniia na poslaniia sv. apostola Pavla: k Galatam* (Moscow, 1893 ), 281.

The sacrament of ordination—"laying on of hands" (Acts 12:3; 1 Tim 4:14; 5:22; 2 Tim 1:6)—is a special gift of God's grace for Christian ministry, through which the gift of the Holy Spirit is given to the Church's bishops and priests in whom the apostolic succession of hierarchy is preserved in the Church. Our Lord Jesus Christ is inseparably one with the Church, as the head is one with the body. He sent His apostles into the world to continue the work of salvation, and that work continues down to the present through His ordained ministers.

S.S. Verhovskoy provided an excellent analysis of this hierarchical authority:

> The Church's hierarchical authority is true and valid only and exclusively in the Church, with the Church, but not over, outside of or in separation from the Church, for then it would be authority over Christ Himself. The Orthodox Church teaches that the fullness of hierarchical authority belongs at all times to Jesus Christ alone, for He alone received full authority from the Father. Jesus entrusted His Church to His Apostles, through whom apostolic succession became established. It is important to remember that hierarchical structure creates of the Church a single organism rather than a chaotic gathering. In the Church there is no place for love of power or personal glory. Only in the heavenly kingdom will God glorify His servants. Authority within the Church consists in service rendered to the Cross of Christ, to the name and in the image of Jesus Christ our King and Redeemer.[4]

The appeal, then, is to follow the example of the Apostle Paul. "I urge you, be imitators of me!" (1 Cor 4:16).

In ordination a person elected by the Church is called to serve all of her members with the special grace of God, by manifesting the power of Christ's own priesthood (Heb 7:24, 26). Recognizing the authority of the apostolic succession of hierarchy, we accept all the rules and regulations of the Church's canonical structure, with the understanding that the Church possesses the authority of Jesus Christ Himself.

---

4  S.S. Verhovskoy, "Sushchnost' vlasti v Tserkvi" in *Tserkovnyi Vestnik* (1951), no. 2.

A call to the priesthood is a call to serve, just as Christ came to serve and not to be served (Mt 20:28). Unlike the lordship exercised by the powerful of this world (Lk 22:25), Christian priesthood involves a highly responsible service for which an answer must be given to God (Acts 20:28; 1 Tim 4:1-14; Jas 3:14-16). For that service is founded on God's own calling (Jn 20:21; Rom 10:15; Heb 5:4).

In the sacrament of marriage the grace of God unites husband and wife in the image of Christ and the Church. This is a union characterized by love, mutual respect, and undefiled purity. The natural union of husband and wife is sanctified by the higher union that exists between Christ and His Church (Eph 5:22-33).[5]

In the eucharist, which is the culminating moment in the life of the Church, we are truly and essentially united with our Lord Jesus Christ Himself (Jn 6:56). The eucharist nourishes our spiritual and physical life (Jn 6:53). In this sacrament, Jesus Christ appears as the cornerstone of our salvation. He makes Himself accessible through the sacrament as our Redeemer and the Redeemer of the world as a whole (1 Jn 2:2). True life in Christ is granted to us only within the Church. Through grace, and especially the gift of Christ's life-giving body and blood. The eucharist manifests the unity of the heavenly and earthly, the living and departed members of the Church.

The eucharist is the sacrament of communion in the body and blood of Christ, for the forgiveness of sins, eternal life, and personal union with God Himself (Jn 6:56-57). The unity of the Church is likewise manifested in the eucharist: "We, being many, are one body, for we all partake of the one bread" (1 Cor 10:17). Accepting Jesus Christ into our heart and soul by a living faith, and receiving His divine life in the holy eucharist, we experience the peace and love of God in our nature as a whole.

5 The Orthodox Christian understanding of marriage is discussed by Prof. Serge Verhovskoy in his book, *The Light of the World* (New York, 1982), 106-107.

St John of Kronstadt explains our eucharistic unity with
Christ in this way:

> Partaking daily of communion in the most holy and life-giving sacra-
> ment, I always felt its life-giving power for my soul and body, felt its vic-
> tory over my sinfulness and death. I became full of joy and gratitude to-
> ward God for permitting me to be a communicant of such a great and
> holy sacrament. I contemplated His mystery: Here is He who is before
> all and by whom all things exist, even the entire universe, for He is be-
> fore all things, and in Him all things consist.[6]

In his Letter 93, St Basil the Great affirms: "I indeed have communion four times a week: Sunday, Wednesday, Friday, Saturday."[7]

Therefore, to live spiritually and morally in God, through Jesus Christ and by the Holy Spirit, and to be blessed by the Holy
Trinity, we must live in the Church which is the true path into the
kingdom of God.

Rejecting and giving up the "old man," while acquiring a new
faith and remaining true to his calling, every Christian, with the
help of the Holy Spirit, begins to grow in spiritual virtues, which
are the "fruit of the Spirit" (Gal 5:22). This involves him in an ongoing struggle, in which he labors diligently and with great effort
against spiritual and physical passions, temptations and desires.
Such Christians belong to Christ, for they believe in Him. They
are united to Him in love, and they take up their Cross and follow
Him (Gal 5:24; Mt 16:24). Thus living by the Spirit, and being
led by the Spirit in his life, thoughts, deeds, feelings and words,
the Christian grows to express the virtues of the Holy Spirit as he
seeks holiness in his personal life.

In the words of St Theophan the Recluse: "Spiritual life is the
greatest source of pure joy. But this joy is not achieved without

---

6   "Sila i slava sviaschenstva" [Power and Glory of the Priesthood] in Vera i Tserkov'
    (1901), vol. 2, 205.
7   St Basil, "Letters and Select Works," in A Select Library of Nicene and Post-Nicene
    Fathers of the Christian Church, (Grand Rapids, 1961).

paying a price. Acquisition of the Holy Spirit is not possible without pain and suffering, or even blood."[8]

The holy Orthodox Church requires holiness of life from her members, in the name of the Holy Trinity. For "He who called you is holy, [therefore] be holy yourselves in all your conduct" (1 Pet 1:15). Recall also the words of St John the Theologian: "Whoever is born of God does not sin, for His seed abides in him, and he cannot sin, because he is born of God" (1 Jn 3:9). In the language of St Paul: "Do you not know that you are the temple of God and that the Spirit of God dwells in you? For the temple of God is holy, which temple you are" (1 Cor 3:16-17). Holiness of life is necessary for every member of Christ's Body (1 Cor 12:27), who constitute living stones of a holy house, a holy priesthood, whose service is to offer sacrifices acceptable to God through Jesus Christ (1 Pet 2:5).

To reach the goal of their calling, all Christians are to lead a spiritual life, "For God did not call us to uncleanness, but to holiness" (1 Thess 4:7). As the Church is presented as a chaste virgin to Christ (2 Cor 11:2), so also the faithful are called to walk worthily of their calling (Eph 4:2), by keeping themselves from the evil one (1 Jn 5:18), by laying aside all filthiness and wickedness, and by receiving the implanted Word by which souls are saved (Jas 2:1). There are things the Christian must flee and refuse to participate in, for if "all things are lawful to me, not all are helpful" (1 Cor 6:12). St Paul enumerates different kinds of sinful actions against God, mankind, and oneself (1 Cor 6:9-10; Eph 5:3-5; Gal 5:19-21). These actions prevent a Christian from entering the kingdom of God. For what fellowship, the apostle asks rhetorically, has light with darkness? (2 Cor 6:14). In another place he recommends: "Pursue peace and holiness with all people, for without these no one will see the Lord" (Heb 12:14).

---

8  *Op. cit.*, "Commentary on Galatians," 412.

Spiritual life is a life of unity with God in prayer, contemplation, truth and love (Eph 6:24; Col 1:6). Every Christian can stand in grace (1 Pet 5:12) and grow in the labor of grace (Eph 3:7-8).

From the Holy Spirit members of Christ's body receive diversities of gifts, according to God's will (1 Cor 12:11), to the measure of Christ's gift (Eph 4:7). And they receive, as well, the "fruit of the Spirit: love, joy, peace, long-suffering, gentleness, goodness, faith, meekness, self-control" (Gal 5:22). Where the Spirit of the Lord is, there is freedom (the liberty of the children of God). And by this same Spirit, we can be transformed from glory to glory (2 Cor 3:17-18).

Love is the primary virtue of the spiritual life: "You shall love the Lord your God with all your heart, with all your soul, with all your mind and with all your strength...and love your neighbor as yourself. On these two commandments hang all the Law and the Prophets" (Mt 22:37-40). Compliance with the Law of God requires that we love one another (Rom 12:8-9). The Lord even commands us to love our enemies, to do good to those who hate us, to bless them and pray for them (Lk 6:27-28). Without Christian love there are no gifts of prophecy, no understanding of mysteries, no true faith—not even if we give our body to be burned, for that will profit us nothing if we do not have love (1 Cor 13:2-3). He who does not love his brother does not know God, for God is love (1 Jn 4:8). Accordingly, love for one another is the sign by which true disciples of Christ will be recognized (Jn 13:35).

The natural, essential expression of love is prayer. The apostle Paul urges first that we offer supplications, prayers, intercessions and thanksgiving for all persons, that we "may lead a quiet and peaceful life, godly and respectful in every way" (1 Tim 2:1-2). If we heed the call of the apostle James, to pray for each other that we may be healed (cf. Jas 5:16), then our Christian love will never end (1 Cor 13:8).

In conclusion, when we are in affliction, wrath, danger and necessity, or when we need healing, the forgiveness of sins, or any kind of help, we know the One to whom we can turn and make our appeal:

"Come to me, all you who labor and are heavy laden, and I will give you rest. Take my yoke upon you and learn from me, for I am gentle and lowly in heart, and you will find rest for your souls. For my yoke is easy and my burden is light" (Mt 11:27-30).

For Orthodox Christians, the first and most essential task is to remain faithful to all that God has granted us within the Church, through our Lord Jesus Christ and the Holy Spirit. This obliges us to be firm and steadfast in adherence to the faith, in participation in the sacraments, and in imitation of the saints in our spiritual and moral lives, so that they might be marked by wisdom, hope and love. This means that we stand fast in God's grace, receiving His gifts without prejudice or pride, and that we discern the spirits, so as to determine the truth that indeed proceeds from God.

Spiritual life in fidelity to God and the Church is accomplished primarily and essentially through the practice of prayer. Prayer is the foundation of the entire spiritual life. Through prayer we accept God's will in our life. For the purpose and goal of prayer is to unite us with God and to fulfill His will, with adoration, thanksgiving, petition, lamentation, and absolute devotion to His service.

The Church's liturgical worship provides us with the content of our spiritual life. It shapes our prayer. Thereby it can create the unique environment in which we think, speak and act, rejecting all that weakens that life and leads us away from its divine purpose and power. We need to receive only what the Church offers us, to practice only what the Church teaches us, and to make our own the saving gifts of the Church.

Rooted in and fortified by the sacramental mysteries of the Church, all Orthodox Christians are to go out into the world to undertake God's mission. They are to make full use of their personal talents and gifts, bestowed by the Holy Spirit. Yet they must do so without spiritual conceit and delusion, without vanity or self-serving pride. Rather, they are to strive constantly to cooperate with the grace of God, in order that through their mission and witness, the divine plan of salvation might become visibly present and powerfully manifested throughout the world.

# Bibliography

Afanasiev, Archpriest N.

1933        Kanony i kanonicheskoe soznanie. *Put'*. Prilozhenie [Appendix].

1934        Dve idei vselenskoi Tserkvi. *Put'* 45:16-29.

1953        Apostol Petr i Rimskii Episkop. *Pravoslavnaia Mysl'* 10:7-31.

1955        *Sluzhenie mirian v Tserkvi*. Paris: Orthodox Theological Institute.

1957        Katholicheskaia Tserkov'. *Pravoslavnaia Mysl'* 11:17-41.

1971        *Tserkov' Dukha Sviatogo*. Paris: YMCA Press.

Afonsky, Priest George

1968        *Pravoslavnoe uchenie o episkope: dogmaticheskoie, sviatootecheskoe, kanonicheskoe*. New York: St Vladimir's Seminary Press.

Aksakov, N.P.

1906        Chto govoriat kakony o sostave Soborov? *Tserkovnyi golos*, nos. 12-15.

Akvilonov, Evgenii

1894        *Tserkov': nauchnyie opredeleniia Tserkvi*. St Petersburg: Tipografia A. Katansky & Co.

Allen, A.

1897        *Christian Institutions*. New York: C. Scribner and Sons.

Athanasius, Saint

1957        *A Select Library of Nicene and Post-Nicene Fathers of the Christian Church*, vol. 4. Grand Rapids, MI: Wm. B. Eerdmans.

Basil the Great, Saint

1901        *Tvorenia svitogo Vasilia Velikogo*. Moscow: Sergiev Posad.

[1957]      *A Select Library of Nicene and Post-Nicene Fathers of the Christian Church*, vol. 8. Grand Rapids, MI: Wm. B. Eerdmans.

Beliaev, A.

1884        *Liubov' bozhestvennaia*. Moscow: [unknown].

Bettenson, H.S. (comp.)

1961        *Documents of the Christian Church*. London: Oxford University Press.

1970        *The Later Christian Fathers: a Selection from the Writings of the Fathers from St Cyril of Jerusalem to St Leo the Great*. London: Oxford University Press.

Bezobrazov, Bishop Kassian

1950        *Khristos i pervoe khristianskoe pokolenie*. Paris: YMCA Press.

Bogdaschevskii, D.
1904        O Tserkvi. *Trudy Kirvskoi Duchovnoi Akademii* 1:167.
Bogolepov, Professor A.A.
1960        Canon Law. *Lectures.* New York: St Vladimir's Seminary Press.
1963        *Which Councils are Recognized as Ecumenical?* New York: St Vladimir's
            Seminary Press.
Bolotov, Professor V.V.
1906        Eparchii v drevnei Tserkvi. *Tserkovnya Vedomosti.* 3.
1907        *Lektsii po istorii drevnei Tserkvi.* St Petersburg: Tipographia M.
            Merkusheva.
Bright, J.
1952        *The Kingdom of God: the Biblical Concept and Its Meaning for the Church.*
            Nashville: Abingdon-Cokesbury Press.
Bulgakov, Archpriest S.N.
1925        Ocherki ucheniia o Tserkvi. *Put',* no. 1.
1925        *Sviatye apostoly Petr i Ioann.* Paris: YMCA Press.
1926        Ocherki ucheniia o Tserkvi. *Put',* nos. 2, 4.
1935        *The Orthodox Church.* London: Centenary Press.
1945        *Nevesta Agntsa.* Paris: YMCA Press.
1965        *Pravoslavie:* ocherki v uchenii Pravoslavnoi Tserkvi. Paris: YMCA Press.
Cummings, D.
1957        *The Rudder (Pedalion) of the Metaphorical Ship of the One Holy Catholic
            and Apostolic Church of Orthodox Christians.* Chicago: Orthodox
            Christian Educational Society.

Cyril, of Jerusalem, Saint
[1956]      *A Select Library of the Nicene and Post-Nicene Fathers of the Christian
            Church,* vol. 7. Grand Rapids, MI: Wm. B. Eerdmans.
Epifanovich, L.
1904        *Zapiski po oblichitel'nomu bogosloviiu.* Novocherkassk: F.M. Tunikova.
Feofan, Saint, Bishop of Tambov and Shatsk [also Theophan, the Recluse]
1892        *Tolkovanie: poslaniia sv. apostola Pavla: k Kolossianam.* Moscow:
            Tipografia I. Efimova.
1893        *Tolkovanie: poslaniia sv. apostola Pavla: k Efeseiam.* Moscow: Tipografia I.
            Efimova.
1893        *Tolkovanie: poslaniia sv. apostola Pavla: k Galatam.* Moscow: Tipografia I.
            Efimova.
Florovsky, Professor Reverend G.V.
1931        *Vostochnyie Ottsy 4 ogo veka.* Paris: Bogoslovskii Institut.
1933        *Vizantiiskie Ottsy 5-ogo po 8-i vek.* Paris: YMCA Press.

1934    Sobornost': the Catholicity of the Church. In *The Church of God*, edited by E.L. Mascall. London: Society for Promoting Christian Knowledge.
1934    The Sacrament of Pentecost. *Journal of the Fellowship of St Alban and St Sergius*, 23.
1934    O granitsakh Tserkvi. *Put'*, no. 44.
1972    *Bible, Church, Tradition: an Eastern Orthodox View*. Belmont, MA: Nordland Publishing Co.

Gette, Priest V.
1881    O vlasti v Tserkvi. *Vera i razum*, March.

Gidulianov, P.
1905    *Mitropolity v pervyie tri veka khristianstva*. Moscow: Universitetskaia Tipographia.

Glubokovskii, Professor N.N.
1910    *Blagovesty sv. Apostola Pavla po ego proiskhozhdeniu i sushchestvu*. St Petersburg.

Gorchakov, Archpriest M.I.
1905    *Tserkovnoe pravo*. St Petersburg:[student, Shiriaev].

Gore, C.
1888    *The Ministry of the Christian Church*. New York: James Pott & Co.

Gorskii, A.V.
1902.    *Istoria evangel'skaia i Tserkvi apostol'skoi*. Moscow: Sergiev Posad.

Grigorii Bogoslov, Saint
1889    *Tvorenia sviatogo Grigoria Bogoslova*. Moscow: Sergiev Posad.

Irenaeus, of Lyons, Saint
1900    *Piat' knig protiv eresi [Five books against heresy]*. Moscow: Sergiev Posad.
[1963]    *The Ante-Nicene Fathers: Translations of the Writings of the Fathers down to AD325*, vol. 1. Grand Rapids, MI: Wm. B. Eerdmans. (A. Roberts & J. Donaldson, eds.).

Jedin, Hubert (editor).
1980-82    *History of the Church*, vol. 1. New York: Crossroad.

John Chrysostom, Saint [Ioann Zlatoust]
1896    *Tvoreniia*. St Petersburg: Dukhovnaia Akademiia.
1956    *A Select Library of the Nicene and Post-Nicene Fathers of the Christian Church*, vol. 13. Grand Rapids, MI: Wm. B. Eerdmans.

John, of Damascus, Saint
1913    *Polnoie sobranie tvorenii*. St Petersburg: Dukhovnaia Akademiia.

John, of Kronstadt, Saint
1901    Sila i slava sviatschenstva. *Vera i Tserkov'*. 2:205.
1894    *Moia zhisn' vo Khriste*. Ithica, NY: Foundation of Fr. John of Kronstadt.

Kartashov, Professor A.V.
1963    *Vselenskie Sobory*. Spain: Osobyi komitet pod predsiedatel'stvom episkopa Sil'vestra.

Kasitsin, D.

1889        Raskoly pervykh vekov khristianstva i vliianie ikh na raskrytie uchenia o
            Tserkvi. *Pribavlenie k Sviatym Otsam.* Moscow, nos. 43, 44.

Katanskii, A.

1877        *Dogmaticheskoe uchenie o semi tserkovnykh tainstvakh.* St Petersburg:
            Tipografia F.G. Eleonskogo.

Kelly, J.N.D.

1960        *Early Christian Doctrines.* New York: Harper & Row.

1963        *A Commentary on the Pastoral Epistles.* New York: Harper & Row.

(Kern), Archimandrite Kyprianos

1947        *Evkharistiia.* Paris: YMCA Press.

Khomiakov, A.S.

1955        *Izbrannye sochineniia.* New York: Chekov Press.

1979        *The Church is One.* New York: St Nectarios Press.

(Khrapovitskii) Metropolitan Antonii

1963        *Nravstvennye idei vazhneishikh khristianskikh pravoslavnykh dogmatov.*
            New York: Diocese of North America and Canada.

Kiparisov, V.

1897        *O tserkovnoi discipline.* Moscow: Sergiev Posad.

Kirk, K.E.

1946        *The Apostolic Ministry: Essays on the History and Doctrine of Episcopacy,*
            London: Hodder & Stoughton.

(Kokkinakis), Bishop Athenagoras

1961        The Hierarchy of the Christian Church. *The Greek Orthodox Theological
            Review* 4:1.

Krasnoschen, Professor M.E.

1907        *Tserkovnoe pravo.* Yuriev: Universitetskaia Tipographia.

Kung, Hans

1967        *The Church.* London: Burns & Oates.

Kurtz, John Henry

1886        *Textbook of Church History.* Philadelphia: J.B. Lippincott Co.

Lebedev, Archpriest A.

1887        *O glavenstve papy: uchenie o Tserkvi.* St Petersburg: Tipografia S. Dobrodeeva.

Lebedev A.P.

1905        *Duchovenstvo drevnei vselenskoi Tserkvi.* Moscow: Tipografia Snegireva.

1906        *Ob uchastii mirian na soborakh.* Moscow: Tipografia Snegireva.

Makarii, Bishop D.B.

1851        Pravoslavno-dogmaticheskoe bogoslovie. St Petersburg: Trusova,
            Tipografia E. Fishera.

Malinovskii, Archpriest N.

1911        *Ocherk pravoslavnogo dogmaticheskogo bogosloviia.* Moscow: Sergiev Posad.
Mansvetov, I.
1879        *Novozavetnoe uchenie o Tserkvi.* Moscow: Tipografia E. Lissner.
Marmion, Dom Columba
1962        *The Structure of God's Plan.* St Louis: B. Herder Book Co.
Mascall, E.L. (editor)
1934        *The Church of God.* London: Society for Promoting Christian Knowledge.
1963        *Christ, the Christian and the Church.* London: Longman, Green & Co., Ltd.
Mersch, Emile
1938        *The Whole Christ: the Historical Development of the Doctrine of the Mystical Body in Scripture and Tradition.* Milwaukee: Bruce Publishing Co.
Meyendorff, Archpriest John
1959        Chto takoe vselenskie Sobory? *Le Messager* 52:10-15.
1960        Ecclesiastical Organization in the History of Orthodoxy. *St Vladimir's Quarterly,* no. 1.
1962        *The Orthodox Church, Its Past and Its Role in the World Today.* New York: Pantheon Books.
1962        Tradition and Traditions. *St Vladimir's Quarterly,* no. 3.
1966        *Orthodoxy and Catholicity.* New York: Sheed & Ward.
1985        *Vvedenie v sviatootecheskoe bogoslovie.* New York: Multi-Lingual Typesetting.
(Milash), Bishop Nikodim
1911        *Pravila Pravoslavnoi Tserkvi s tolkovaniiami,* vols. 1, 2. St Petersburg: St Petersburg Theological Academy.

Molchanov, Priest Aleksei
1888        *Sv. Kyprian Karfagenskii i ego uchenie o Tserkvi.* Kazan: Imperial University.
Myschtsin, V.
1905        Naskol'ko obiazatelen avtoritet tserkovnykh kanonov? *Bogoslovskii Vestnik.* 3:816-823.
1908        Tserkovnoe ustroistvo po poslaniam Sviatogo Ignatia Bogonostsa. *Bogoslovskii Vestnik,* 5-7.
1909        *Ustroistvo khristianskoi Tserkvi v pervye dva veka.* Moscow: Sergiev Posad.
Nechaev, P.
1895        *Prakticheskoe rukovodstvo dlia sviashchennosluzhitelei.* St Petersburg: House of the Poor Children.
Pavlov, A.S.
1902        *Kurs Tserkovnogo prava.* Moscow: Sergiev Posad.
Pokrovskii, A.I.
1915        *Sobory drevnei Tserkvi.* Moscow: Sergiev Posad.

Pokrovskii, Aleksei
1891    Pravoslavno-khristianskoe nravstvennoe bogoslovie. Samara: Tipografia
        N.A. Zhdanova.
Ponomarev, P.P.
1908    *Sviashchennoe predanie, kak istochnik Khristianskogo vedeniia*. Kazan:
        Tsentral'naia Tipografia.
Popkov, A.A.
1911    Pisaniia muzhei apostolskikh. *Bogoslovskii Vestnik.*
Prat, F.
1950    *Jesus Christ: His Life, His Teaching, and His Work*, vols. 1, 2. Milwaukee:
        Bruce Publishing Co.
1961    *Theology of St Paul*, vols. 1, 2. Westminster, MD: Newman Press.
Preobrazhenskii, P.
1895    *Pisania muzhei apostolskikh.* St Petersburg: Lopuchin.
Quasten, Johannes
1949    *Patrology*, vols. 1, 2, 3. Westminster, MD: Newman Press.
Roberts, Reverend Alexander and James Donaldson (editors)
1963    *The Ante-Nicene Fathers: Translations of the Writings of the Fathers down to
        AD325,* 10 vols. Grand Rapids, MI: Wm. B. Eerdmans.
Samarin, Fedor
1908    *Pervonachal'naia khristianskaia Tserkov' v Ierusalime.* Moscow.
Schaff, Phillip and Henry Wage (editors)
1971    *A Select Library of the Nicene and Post-Nicene Fathers of the Christian
        Church,* 14 vols. Grand Rapids, MI: Wm. B. Eerdmans.
Schmemann, Archpriest Alexander
1949    Tserkov' i tserkovnoie ustroistvo. *Tserkovnyi Vestnik* (Z.E.P.E.R).
1953    *O Tserkvi: Pravoslavie v zhizni.* New York: Chekov Press.
1954    *Istoricheskii put' pravoslaviia.* New York: Chekov Press.
1960    Primacy and Primacies in the Orthodox Church. *St Vladimir's Quarterly,*
        nos. 2-3.
1963    *Report to the All-American Council.* In the Archives of the Orthodox
        Church in America.
1965    *Sacraments and Orthodoxy.* New York: Herder and Herder.
1974    *Of Water and the Spirit: A Liturgical Study of Baptism.* New York: St
        Vladimir's Seminary Press.
1983    *Za zhizn' mira.* New York: St Vladimir's Seminary Press.
1988    *The Eucharist–Sacrament of the Kingdom.* New York: St Vladimir's
        Seminary Press.
Schnackenburg, R.
1963    *God's Rule and Kingdom.* New York: Herder and Herder.
1965    *The Church in the New Testament,* New York: Herder and Herder.

(Sokolov), Bishop Ioann

1859    *Opyt kursa tserkovnogo zakonovedenia.* St Petersburg: Tipografia F.G. Eleonskogo.

1877    *Dogmat o Presviatoi Troitse.* St Petersburg: Tipografia F.G. Eleonskogo.

Solertinskii, Archpriest P.

1884    *Opyt bibleiskogo slovaria.* St Petersburg: [unknown].

Soloviov, V.

1958    *Dukhovnye osnovy zhizni.* New York: Fordham University.

Spasskii, A.

1914    *Istoriia dogmaticheskikh dvizhenii v epochu vselenskikh Soborov.* Moscow: Sergiev Posad.

(Stragorodskii), Archimandrite Sergii

1894    *Pravoslavnoie uchenie o spasenii.* Moscow: Sergiev Posad.

Suvorov, N.

1913    *Uchebnik tserkovnogo prava.* Moscow: Tipografia Ia. Dankin i Ia. Khomutov.

Swete, H.B.

1910    *The Holy Spirit in the New Testament: A Study of Primitive Christian Teaching.* London: Macmillan and Co., Ltd.

1920    *Essays on the Early History of the Church and the Ministry.* London: Macmillan and Co., Ltd.

(Tikhomirov) Metropolitan Sergii of Japan

1935    *Dvenadtsat' sviatykh apostolov.* Paris: YMCA Press.

(Troitskii), Archimandrite Ilarion.

1954    *Khristianstva net bez Tserkvi.* São Paulo: Brotherhood of St Job.

Troitskii, Vladimir.

1913    *Ocherki iz istorii dogmata o Tserkvi.* Moscow: Sergiev Posad.

[Unknown], Bishop Sylvester

1872    *Uchenie o Tserkvi v pervie tri veka khristianstva.* Kiev: Tipografia G.T. Korchak-Novitskogo.

1872    *Uchenie o Tserkvi soborov v donikeiskii period.* Kiev: Tipografia G.T. Korchak-Novitskogo.

1897    *Opyt pravoslavnogo dogmaticheskogo bogosloviia.* Kiev: Tipografia G.T. Korchak-Novitskogo.

[Unknown]

1723    *Message of the Patriarchs of the Eastern-Catholic Church About the Orthodox Faith* (1723), no. 2. [Ecumenical Patriarch, Jeremiah].

1848    *General Message of the One, Holy, Catholic and Apostolic Church to All Orthodox Christians* (1848) [Ecumenical Patriarch Anfim].

[Unknown]

1884    *Pravila sviatykh Apostolov, vselenskikh soborov, pomestnykh soborov, sviatykh ottsov s tolkovaniami.* Moscow: Tipografia L.F. Snegireva.

Verkhovskoy, S.S.

1951    Sushchnost' vlasti v Tserkvi. *Tserkovnyi Vestnik* (Z.E.P.E.R), no. 2.

1953    *Bog i chelovek.* New York: Chekov Press.

1953    Pravoslavie v zhizni: Khristos i Khristianstvo. *In Sbornik statei.* New York: Chekov Press.

1982    *The Light of the World: Essays on Orthodox Christianity.* New York: St Vladimir's Seminary Press.

Voronov, Archpriest Liverii

1994    *Dogmaticheskoe bogoslovie.* Moscow: Khronika [Moscow Patriarchate].

Yastrebov, M.

1902    Chto takoi Tserkov'? *Trudy Kievskoi Dukhovnoi Akademii,* vol. 1. Kiev: Tipografia I.I. Gorbunovo.

Zaozerskii, N.A.

1894    *O Tserkovnoi vlasti.* Moscow: Sergiev Posad.

1909    O sushchnosti Tserkovnogo prava. *Bogoslovskii Vestnik* 3:313-577.

1911    Ierarkhicheskii printsip v tserkovnoi organizatsii. *Bogoslovskii Vestnik* 1:64-103.

Zernov, Professor N.

1933    Sviatoi Kiprian Karfagenskii i edinstvo vselenskoi Tserkvi. *Put'*.

Zohm, R.

1906    *Tserkovnyi stroi v pervyie tri veka khristianstva.* Moscow: [unknown].

## Bibles consulted

King James Version

1982    *The Holy Bible.* Nashville: Thomas Nelson Publication.

1992    *The Bible, Old and New Testament* (In Russian). Moscow: Rossiiskoe Bibleiskoe Obshchestvo.

1993    *The Orthodox Study Bible* (New Testament). Nashville: St Athanasius Orthodox Academy.

## Other

1934    *The Orthodox Prayer Book.* Wilkes-Barre, PA: The Russian Orthodox Catholic Mutual Aid Society of the United States of America.